Acknowledg

dedicate this book to my dear and f...er
...is journey would never have been u...ay
...und as though Jean was the one w...
...NITE refreshments! However, most
...nes from beginning to end. Not only that, but the inspiration God
...ave was given jointly and the great blessing received was shared
...etween us. Thank you, Father God, for Your gift of unity which we
...ave endeavoured to celebrate through over 100 UNITE events.

...any have undertaken this journey with us and friends and
...pporters have multiplied along the way. For this we are truly
...ankful to God. He has been a constant source of strength and
...ncouragement and we have acknowledged Him at every opportunity.
...'s beyond my mental capacity to mention everyone who helped us
...get going, supported us along the way and encouraged us through
...fficult times (and there have been some!) I believe it would be true
...say that the nucleus of Stoke-on-Trent Christians who joined us at
...e beginning were those we got to know through the late Harold
...oodwin who was a great 'connector' of people in addition to being an
...tremely talented musician. His composition 'Crucified before
...reation' was a choir piece which was taken around the whole area of
...orth Staffordshire. I had the honour of being the narrator for all the
...rformances of this musical and evangelical outreach. Many of the
...oir members came along to our early UNITE events and have
...ntinued ever since.

...e are extremely grateful to our original seven 'Pillars'! God gave
...e a vision of a platform coming down from heaven and all he
...quired from us was to support it, giving Jesus 'centre-stage'. We
...lled our team 'Pillars' – they supported the platform. Their help,
...pport and friendship was invaluable and we wish to express our
...atitude here. They were Joan Adams, Ann Grainger, Lee and Lydia
...lmer and Cliff and Lottie Roberts – plus Jean and myself. If that
...akes eight, God added one for good measure!

...everyone else, "Thank you!" Really this has been a joint effort.
...u have all been part of this. So please read on. I hope you will be
...essed!

UNITE
The Journey

By Cedric Barber

Published for Cedric Barber by
Verité CM Limited,
124 Sea Place, Worthing, West Sussex BN12 4BG
+44 (0) 1903 241975

email: enquiries@veritecm.com
Web: www.veritecm.com

British Library Cataloguing in Publication Data
A catalogue record for this book is available from the British Library

Design and Print Management by Verité CM Ltd

Cover design by Carl Scott

Printed in England

CONTENTS

Now may God, the source of great endurance and comfort, grace you with UNITY among yourselves, which flows from your relationship with Jesus, the Anointed One. Then, with a unanimous rush of passion, you will with one voice glorify God, the Father of our Lord Jesus Christ.

Romans 15:5-6 The Passion Translation

FOREWORD

There are UK ministries that carry such an anointing as the gospel is presented. UNITE Ministries led by Jean and Cedric Barber is up there with the best of them.

People from all denominations are invited to these down-to-earth, spirit-led, no jargon meetings which include testimony from people who don't normally get an opportunity to share.

This book traces the history of UNITE and will bring you great encouragement as you read stories from real people of God.

Peter Gladwin
CEO Out of Ashes Ministries

INTRODUCTION

As a prelude to this book, I'd like to offer this light-hearted introduction:

A Christian has been stranded on a desert island by himself for many years. He is rescued one day, and the rescuers are confused to see that he has built two churches. They ask him why. Pointing to one of them, he replies, "Well that's the church that I go to." Pointing to the other, he says, "And that's the one I don't go to!"

Sounds nonsensical doesn't it, but if you find it mildly amusing you will already have an awareness of the way many churchgoers are seen to view their places of worship – certainly in the UK. I don't exclude North Staffordshire because it is the area from which this book is drawn.

This is a book about nine years of meetings called 'UNITE', the aim of which was to bring Christians together, to ENCOURAGE them, to CONNECT them and to INTRODUCE others to Jesus! You will read about the vision, the practical difficulties, the opposition but above all, the excitement and satisfaction of being led by God to put on these monthly events around the country.

2011 was an exciting year for my wife, Jean and me. It was the year we began 'UNITE', a series of monthly events for Christians to connect together, worship God, give testimony of Jesus in their lives and for non-Christians to join in and have an opportunity to discover who this man, Jesus really is! In fact, the whole of the New Millennium has been exciting for us and for many others too!

Mine and Jean's journey together began with our marriage in September 2000. At the time of writing that was twenty years ago this month. We were ministering together in a number of churches but not seeing any visible response. Then in 2004, on our first visit to a Hollybush Christian Centre meeting in North Yorkshire (also known as 'Miracle Valley and 'The Church on a Farm') we were given a remarkable and life-changing prophecy. The Pastor, Jim Wilkinson together with a man who appeared out of the congregation, spoke over our lives. The exact words were "You shall go from town to town in England to give out the Gospel message of Jesus Christ (take your Bibles with you!) and afterwards people will come up to you and ask about it." We were thrilled as this was completely unexpected.

In the two years that followed, very little of spiritual significance happened, but I believe God was working in the background and preparing our way forward in His service. Do you believe that God does this in your life? Do you believe He has a plan for your life? Let me explain. Around the same time I watched a Channel 4 documentary where I was surprised to see my cousin, Dennis Barber, presenting the results of years of his meticulous research into the Barber family history. I discovered that all my forebears on my father's side were black, going back just two generations. In fact seven generations back, my direct 4xgreat grandfather was a black slave boy in Jamaica. His name was Quashey. His owner, a certain Captain Bathurst, brought him to England as his own servant, but owing to social and financial difficulties, he 'gave him away'. By this time, Quashey had been 'Christianised' and given the name Francis Barber. The recipient of this now ten year old black boy turned out to be no other than the famous and revered literary giant of the 18th Century, Doctor Samuel Johnson. Among many other high ideals, Dr Johnson was a philanthropist, a high churchman and an outspoken opponent of the infamous Slave Trade which was in full swing during that time. To say the least, I was intrigued. The excitement was to follow. I began to do a little of my own research and discovered that Francis had a son called Samuel 'who was a preacher of note in North Staffordshire'. I went on to find out that Sam was the 'first black preacher in the Primitive Methodist Revival'. As I discovered more about Sam, I began to feel a very emotional connection to him. He was my own flesh and blood, my family, a much admired Christian man who had lived and died in my home town of Tunstall, Stoke-on-Trent. We'll hear a little more about grandad Sam early in Chapter 5. Although a poor man working in the Pottery industry 14 hours a day, he led many men and women to a saving relationship with Jesus Christ. Because of this Christian revival sweeping the Potteries at that time another consequence was an upsurge in moral, social and educational standards of the people.

This information, although well known in the Barber family had been 'hidden in plain sight'! It seemed that in my generation I was the one to make it known, and in 2008 I published a history of the Barber family with an emphasis on its spiritual impact, 'Slaves, Sinners and Saints'. My new knowledge certainly propelled me into a closer walk with God. I was emotionally, physically and spiritually charged with energy to see God move wherever Jean and I ministered. It was exciting! I believe this was a filling with the Holy Spirit like Peter experienced at Pentecost! I began to get involved with the African churches. I loved Africans and Caribbeans and just wanted to identify with them. They warmly accepted me and this white man felt greatly humbled by their love.

Another life-changing adventure began in 2011; I was retired early, put out to graze! This meant that for the first time in my life I had time on my hands. However, I believe that when God's Holy Spirit has His way it is always at the right time in the right place with the right people. At this time Jean began talking about things we'd heard in the Pentecostal churches we were involved in. Some of the older folks said, "There's nothing for Christians to do on a Saturday night. In the old days Christians from all the churches used to meet on Saturday nights and enjoy fellowship and praising God." Jean felt inspired to 'bring on back the good times' by holding a similar sort of meeting. She told our friends George and Jane Smith who passed this on to their pastor, Robert Mountford. Robert is now the Ecumenical Mission Officer for Staffordshire and the Potteries and also a good friend with a multitude of Christian contacts and much influence in the North Staffordshire churches. He encouraged us tremendously considering we had never done anything like this before, and on 18th July, 2011, Jean and I met with Robert and his two church elders, Mike Bright and Jean McLellan in Crossroads Church within the Cardway factory in Alsager. Unbeknown to us they had been praying for some sort of outreach to be held in their church on a Saturday evening. They felt that our idea of a Saturday night meeting was just what they wanted to bring in Christians from across the area. The fact that 'Crossroads Church' met in a factory and not in a church building sat well with me because I didn't want the different church denominations to feel uncomfortable. An evangelist friend of mine once said he didn't agree with all the different 'abominations'! Of course, he meant 'denominations'. This was to be a non-denominational and interdenominational venture.

So it was that Jean and I settled on the name 'UNITE' for the event and we arranged for the first meeting to take place at 7pm on

Saturday 24th September, 2011 in the Cardway factory. This was exactly nine years ago today at the time of writing. Right time, right place, right people! The following chapters relate to our new lease of life which began to revolve around regular Saturday evening UNITE events which, in turn, became increasingly popular over the years. We saw Christians from many different backgrounds come together under the headship of Jesus enjoying God's gift of unity to His people. We saw people make friendships and connections, we saw people reconciled to one another, we saw many, many people make first-time commitments to Jesus and we saw people healed in the meetings in answer to prayer. A notable example was a young lady who was prayed for and received sight in her blind eye. We introduced evangelists to many local churches and got to know a good number of young people who were passionate about making the name of Jesus known in the towns and cities of our nation. Yes, we were excited and there was a growing number of Christians who were also excited and pleased to come on board to help us. As time went on we began Saturday morning evangelism outreach in the local towns with followers of UNITE. Then around three years ago we set up six-monthly Pastors and Ministry Leaders Breakfast Meetings. These drew in ministers from all denominations locally and got them working together.

All glory goes to God, we could never have envisaged any of this happening. We had no special talent, only a desire to be obedient. Jean's gift was providing food and fellowship, mine was networking and encouraging people. Together we put on 107 Saturday evening events over eight-and-a-half years in five different counties and we saw God do amazing things. I pray the following seven chapters will inspire you to know that God has given you gifts and He is interested in seeing you use them. If God's people will make themselves available and remain obedient to His calling, there is no limit to what He will do; especially if we do it in UNITY!

FIRST STEPS

'Do not despise these small beginnings, for the lord rejoices to see the work begin..'
Zechariah 4:10

7pm Saturday 24th September arrived. Our very first UNITE event took place in the Cardway factory. I'm going to devote this short first chapter to this event as it's one I will always remember. Many events followed, but this first meeting was significant for a number of reasons. One reason was that we didn't know if anyone would turn up! I had asked my sister to come and invited many from our own church, Biddulph Pentecostal, plus Christians we had got to know from across Stoke-on-Trent. I have since discovered that it is quite an achievement to get folks out of their homes on a Saturday evening! Being late September it was beginning to get dark in the run up to 7pm. Of course, most Christians think of 7.30pm as the 'official time' for evening meetings, so some didn't arrive until then. A trickle of people entered the upstairs meeting room as Jean and I kept looking out into the gloom to see if there were any more arrivals. The Cardway factory is in a remote place and we wondered if folks would be able to find us. As we were in industrial premises Jean had to keep a record of people attending. We still have the list which shows 40 adults and seven children.

Eventually we were pleasantly surprised with the number of folks, 27 of whom came from various churches around North

Staffordshire. Since I mentioned my African connection in the Introduction, it's interesting to note that we had families who came representing Nigeria, Zambia, Zimbabwe and Jamaica – plus quite a number of English! Jason Challinor from our own church came to help with leading worship and he brought all his family with him. Jason has always been ready to help with electronics and support generally whenever we've asked. So our worship band and sound system were ready to go. The sound system is often the biggest complication just before our events begin and can take my attention away from welcoming people, spending time with our speakers and most importantly getting a prayer group together to ask God to have His way in the meeting. But all went well and we were ready to start.

I introduced the meeting by asking for prayer from the floor. Then I gave the reason for the meeting. It was simply 'Connecting and encouraging Christians; Introducing people to Jesus' and to give Him first place in our gatherings. Our desire was that Christians would go back to their respective churches the next day filled with joy and excitement! This statement later became the slogan we used on all our advertising and media. Then the band struck up in lively praise and worship. It is beautiful to praise the Lord! This created an atmosphere to welcome the Holy Spirit in to guide us through 'uncharted territory'! Next, people were invited to share what Jesus had done in their lives to encourage others, and this provokes more testimonies as folks become bolder. We were encouraged!

One thing we learned to pre-empt at every meeting was folks getting on the platform and preaching. We have Christians come along from many different denominations and peripheral differences in doctrine and understanding or overemphasis on personal opinions and denominational traditions can rankle with folks. We say "The testimony of Jesus is the Spirit of prophecy". We always look for testimony which will bless and encourage folks and if prophecy is involved we look for confirmation. However, it's not easy to control this when everyone is given the opportunity to speak. This was not a problem in our first event. But here's a little story I sometimes relate to try and emphasise this.

A pastor who had just retired decided that he would like to do some missionary work. He'd preached to his own congregation for years and they never took much notice. He couldn't understand why, and felt they didn't appreciate his preaching qualities. The Mission Board sent him to a remote village in Africa where he was warmly welcomed by the chief who got all the villagers together so that the pastor could preach to them. He began preaching. He was surprised by the level of response among the villagers as he spoke. They kept excitedly shouting "Mgumbo, Mgumbo" throughout his sermon. He was sure they must be really delighted with his message. Afterwards the chief took him back to his accommodation which was the best hut in the village standing in its own field. The chief explained that the hut was excellent, but advised the pastor to be careful as he walked through the field as a herd of cows had just been there. The Chief warned him, "Make sure you don't step in any mgumbo!"

I'm reasonably confident we had no 'mgumbo' during our meeting!

What has become an important part of these UNITE events then followed. The interval! This is where Jean comes into her own. She makes our guests welcome as she provides food and drink for everyone. This time of fellowship is so important and we let it continue for up to half an hour. To adapt the words of an old friend from our church, "Just like the love of the Lord, food and fellowship are entirely free!" This was so important to us. We didn't want anyone to feel they couldn't get along to these events because of lack of money. We decided from the beginning that we would provide quite substantial refreshments plus admission to all our events entirely free of charge. We have continued with this policy even when the rental of premises, the cost of speakers/evangelists and their accommodation and transport has been burdensome. Having said this, we have been surprised by the generosity of some people who have given us a gift or supported us with accommodation or transport for our speakers or praise band. So often we have set off in our car to an event only able to squeeze in one extra passenger because all spare space was taken up with hot water pots and food! We realised we were taking part in something special.

And so the 'second half' followed after the interval. We had arranged for our friends from church, Jamie and Melanie Bouton to be interviewed by Linda Reeves about their lives, how they came to meet with Jesus and what it was in their lives that had changed because of Him. It was interesting, holding everyone's attention and it worked well. This sort of forum is able to bring out feelings and unusual and unexpected situations which only in hindsight can be explained by divine intervention. I gave no appeal for people to respond to the Gospel message of Salvation in Jesus at the end of the evening. I was quite used to making such appeals and was later criticised for not doing so, but I'm thrilled that I didn't! I believe the Holy Spirit was free to move in this meeting. I also believe that for me to have done so would have stifled (or quenched) the Holy Spirit in His design for the evening. The reason I say this is that shortly after the end of the meeting an eight year old boy, of his own freewill, made a serious commitment to follow Jesus Christ as his Lord and Saviour. The boy was Micah Boulton, the son of our speakers for the evening. He had never heard his parents talk like this before. He said "Being a Christian sounds exciting!" Mum and Dad didn't want to force anything on him and left him to make his own decision. This he did at our very first UNITE event. I was thrilled, Micah was thrilled and his parents were thrilled. Everyone who knew him was thrilled, not to mention the angels rejoicing in heaven!

So this was our first event. People turned up. The Holy Spirit turned up. Salvation came to that factory on 24th September 2011. I truly believe that what happened was God's stamp of approval on the UNITE initiative. If you feel you can read through the next few chapters you'll hear more about Micah as a 16 year old Christian following Jesus with passion!

CHAPTER 2

THE EARLY JOURNEY

*'Jesus went through the cities and villages, teaching and
journeying towards Jerusalem.'*
Luke 13:22

Boyed up by our first momentous event, we pressed on with our journey from one town to another (remember that Hollybush prophecy?), managing to avoid meeting in church buildings. We held UNITE events each month without fail in a café, community centre, United Christian Broadcasters dining room, village hall, hotel and even a church hall. Then we seemed to run out of non-church premises! As you will discover, we found that non-Christians were quite willing to come into churches on a Saturday night, so why shouldn't Christians? It wasn't a problem. The format and freedom everyone enjoyed in the meetings and the reality of the testimonies (not to mention the food!) made it so easy for us to put on this 'platform' – more about the 'platform' later! Jean and I were definitely on a learning curve and we were journeying to somewhere special and gathering support as we went. God was blessing this calling He had given us.

At the very beginning, we decided to set out a brief statement of what we were doing under the UNITE banner. Here is the statement:

UNITE is a group of believers with a passion to celebrate harmony and unity among Christians whatever their background and to introduce people to JESUS – giving Him FIRST PLACE!

Here are some of the ways we go about this:

- Holding regular Saturday evening events throughout Stoke-on-Trent and beyond where everyone is encouraged to share their Christian testimony and people are introduced to JESUS. Lively modern Christian worship. Anointed Christian speakers from all walks of life.
- Saturday morning outings into local towns to share the love of Jesus with people.
- Six-monthly Pastors/Ministry Leaders Breakfast meetings
- Encouraging, supporting and introducing Christians and Christian Ministries to one another, bringing together strategic partners in God's Kingdom.
- Linking and getting to know local churches by visiting them, worshipping God with them and making friends.
- Promoting love and harmony in Jesus' name.

Cedric & Jean Barber Co-founders of UNITE

www.christiansunite.org.uk 07815 830123

We based this on Psalm 133:

How good and pleasant it is when God's people live together in unity! . . . For there the Lord bestows his blessing, even life for evermore.

And John 17:21:

Jesus prayed " . . . that all of them may be one, Father, just as you are in me and I am in you. May they also be in us so that the world may believe that you have sent me."

Although we were criticised for having a Saturday night Christian 'knees-up' which would be of no value, we strongly believed that it was not for us to create unity, but that it is a gift from God to believers, the Body of Christ, and will be consummated in heaven. Our purpose was for Christians to celebrate that unity. The Apostle Paul makes a significant statement in Ephesians 4:5-6 where he contends that in the Church of Jesus Christ there is only *one* body, *one* Spirit, *one* hope, *one* Lord, *one* faith, *one* baptism and one God and Father over all.

Our desire was for Christians to believe and receive this oneness, this unity, in the same way as they had received their salvation through Jesus Christ – by faith. We saw the fulfilment of these verses many times. Christians were being healed and reconciled to one another (blessed). People from the 'world' (unbelievers), came to our meetings and realised that God had sent Jesus and they committed their lives to Him.

Over the next year or so we held around fourteen UNITE events in three different counties, Staffordshire, Cheshire and Lancashire, though the majority were in and around Stoke-on-Trent. In this chapter I just want to dwell on this particular season because it was all new to us: seeing prayers answered, seeing people healed, testimony from mature spirit-filled Christians, miracles and getting involved with so many Christians at the forefront of God's work and the various churches along the way. We were privileged and we were enjoying it!

A month later, at the end of October, we held UNITE in the café adjacent to Swan Bank Church in Burslem. This is the town where Jean and I were born. It is also the town where all my Barber forebears were born going back to Sam Barber the evangelist. Like Sam, most of them were black. Someone said that it was the shock of marrying English ladies down the generations that turned us white!

The café is not large and the 45 folks who came along filled the place. There was a buzz of excitement as we began. Two incidents are memorable. Lottie Roberts was experiencing severe pain in her face. We decided that everyone in the room should pray for her. While we were praying people said that they saw Lottie's face changing shape. She was healed there and then. Glory to God! Then Dave Garner, his daughter Lydia and her husband, Lee, all leaders of nearby St John's Church in Burslem, asked for prayer for their protection. This was 29th October and on the 31st Halloween is celebrated by many folks who are drawn to St John's because of the siting of the grave of Molly Lee. Molly was said to be a witch who, after her death, haunted several premises in Burslem including the Leopard pub just up the road from our venue. Her grave, instead of lying in an east-west direction, normal for Christian burial, lies in a north-south direction. It is easily found. Dave Garner told us that they hold a half-night prayer vigil in the church on Halloween. In the past they had experienced children with their parents visiting the grave early in the evening. Later in the evening when the pubs turned out they had windows in the church smashed. However, their real concern and the one for which they asked for prayer was what happened in the early hours when some weird characters visited. Dave told us that they had actually received death threats from Satanists and witches in the past. Again we prayed collectively for our friends from St John's. This was the beginning of a friendship with our brothers and sisters in that historic church. History reveals that the world-famous pottery manufacturer, Josiah Wedgwood was baptised there and another famous potter, Enoch Wood is buried there. Another item of interest is that Sam Barber attended the church before his conversion! Just to add to this, I have always put an article in the local newspaper, 'The Sentinel', reporting the events of the meetings. In response to the article I received an anonymous letter explaining that witches didn't exist and another anonymous one criticising me for starting a 'new religion'. Interesting, isn't it that, though the devil is real, he too, prefers to remain anonymous!

One more event followed before Christmas 2011. This was held in the Cornerstone Community Centre in Silverdale. The Centre which was formerly a school, had been bought by the Elim Church in Silverdale where a beautiful man of God, Edwin Cotter, was the Pastor. Up to this point we had encountered some opposition to the idea that different church denominations should happily meet together enjoying the Lord's presence and each other's on a Saturday evening. This had been mainly from people in church leadership. Edwin was totally the opposite. I'll never forget just after this meeting Edwin coming to us and saying, "Your church is the other side of North Staffordshire, but we're here for you". A diametrically opposed attitude to one or two of our critics. At the time of writing, many who knew Edwin will be aware that he has now gone to be with his Lord and Saviour, Jesus Christ, following his death from Coronavirus. Our loss is heaven's gain! The number of people attending UNITE had now risen to around 60. Ann Grainger was our main speaker. Her testimony was very moving and we later began to be involved more and more with Ann's ministry. Significantly the St John's folks came along and reported back on the result of our prayers at the previous meeting. Halloween that year had been one of the quietest they had ever experienced! Thank you Lord!

We moved into 2012 and held seven UNITE events before taking a break in August. January's event was in the UCB Dining Hall when Jon and Heather Bellamy of Cross Rhythms Radio spoke for us. We had some beautiful praise and worship led by a 12 strong group of young singers from the Redeemed Christian Church of God (RCCG) in Stoke. Many folks who have come to UNITE will be aware that I have been known to strike up a song; sometimes people join in! On this occasion my 'Bless the Lord Oh my Soul' found spontaneous accompaniment from behind me as the group sang in harmony and power! What a blessing! Many were prayed for at the end of the evening.

February found us back in Cornerstone Community Centre when Tom Buckett's mum, Mandy, spoke about his amazing recovery from near death after falling from a roof. According to the doctors he should have died. His skull was pushed half way through his brain! But people prayed. He should then have become a 'cabbage' not knowing his parents. But people prayed. He should then not have been able to walk. But people prayed. These are facts, but they are not the whole truth. The Bible asks "Who has believed our report?" Was Mandy to believe the doctors when so many Christians were praying for Tom's healing? Or was she going to believe God's report? Later the same year when the London Olympics were held, Tom ran through nearby Cobridge carrying the Olympic Torch! A miracle! Glory to God. There were two other reports. Our friend George Smith testified of the surprise of his doctor after a cancer fell off his hand and Doreen Adams told how her reflux problem/ hiatus hernia had been healed. These two friends were prayed for at the previous UNITE event.

These monthly Saturday evening events continued through March into April. In March we were at Tunstall Methodist Church Hall – we turned down the offer of the church! A lady with an amazing testimony, Jean Lupton from Nottingham, was our guest speaker. At the April event we met in Scholar Green Village Hall. This was significant as it was the new venue for the Crossroads Church, the one which we partnered with at our first event in the Cardway factory. By this stage, we were beginning to get around 70 folks come along to the meetings. The Village Hall was packed! I recorded: *'Excitement mounted from the start as we heard 'ordinary people' tell of God's extraordinary provision for them and the seemingly impossible opportunities they had received to speak about Jesus in the preceding weeks.'* Lee Plummer, a local curate was our speaker and he thrilled us with stories of his former work with orphans in China. Lee spoke out a scripture to encourage us. It was Ephesians 3 verse 20. Keep reading and discover how this was to increase one man's faith sufficient for him to receive an astonishing miracle of healing! There was much ministry going on during the interval and we were privileged to have Harold and Jean Allender from Devon help us with this.

Spring was turning into summer as we met in Penkhull Christian Centre, our first event in church premises. This was in May 2012 and our speaker was the inimitable John Holme of Operation Great Britain. John had been on the 'Richard and Judie' show recently following his flying over London in a hang-glider while speaking the gospel through a megaphone! He was prosecuted for low flying! Around 90 people turned up for this meeting and some great testimony was enjoyed. A young lady responded to the gospel call and committed her life to Jesus at the end of the evening. We thanked Pastor Marcus Chilaka for stepping in to save the evening with the 'Golden Voices' from his church (RCCG, Stoke) after our planned worship leader had to call off with flu. Nigerian worship is very 'inclusive'. I mean it doesn't take much for the whole congregation to join in when someone starts a chorus off. However, we had an English congregation here, but I wasn't going to be put off! I decided on a favourite chorus of theirs where they I started off

"Who is greater than Jehovah Lord divine. . ." The ladies responded in song *"There is no-one greater than Jehovah Lord divine."* Absolutely brilliant! Another church, this time St John's in Burslem hosted us for our June event. This was warm and homely in spite of the age of the church and our friends Dave, Lydia and Lee made us very welcome. The Holy Spirit was also very welcome in our gathering. I made an appeal and a lady made a decision for Jesus. She was to be baptised a few weeks later. Speakers were Tony Green from Leek and Michelle Fahey from Silverdale.

July found us back at the Cornerstone Community centre in Silverdale. This was our tenth UNITE meeting and we combined it with a barbeque. Cliff Roberts and Tunde Abraham were chefs for the evening. They did a brilliant job. As soon as we got the barbeque going it began to rain! However the indoor facilities at the centre were great and no-one got too wet even though someone said it was raining cats and hot dogs! The evening went well with much testimony and ministry. Speakers were Tim Leech and Ken Espley. People were beginning to realise that they could bring their needs to these events, be ministered to, prayed for and receive the joy of the Lord Jesus. Quoting Chapter One, 'Our desire was that Christians would go back to their respective churches the next day filled with joy and excitement!'

We were now in August, 2012. Jean's birthday is in August and we have managed to keep the month clear of meetings most years. This year we stayed for a week in beautiful Reeth, Swaledale, in North Yorkshire. It was quiet and peaceful and we enjoyed the Sunday morning meeting at the Evangelical Church in the heart of the village where we made a few friends and later walked along the banks of the River Swale. A lovely break. One year in Reeth we joined with the Reeth Brass Band and a village green full of folks singing hymns and hearing some preaching from the ministers of the local churches. Hallelujah, I love to hear the word of God preached in the open air. At the end of the service we moved from the spiritual to the aesthetic and sung the Anthem of Reeth:

I will sing of a place that is dear to my heart
A place where I always would dwell,
And if you will kindly lend me your ear
A few of its beauties I'll tell
Chorus: Beautiful dale, home of the Swale,
How well do I love thee, how well do I love thee?
Beautiful dale, home of the Swale,
Beautiful, beautiful dale

Local people sing it church and some sing it in pubs, but many will know I love to take songs and put some of my own words to them to sing at UNITE. I use the word 'sing' advisedly! I thought, what about:

'I will sing of a place that is dear to my heart,
A place that I always would dwell,
Beautiful Zion, home of the Lord
Beautiful, beautiful Zion'

We love Yorkshire and always visit Hollybush Christian Centre in Thirsk where we received our prophecy over eight years previously (see Introduction). We never fail to visit Hollybush, 'The Church on a Farm'/'Miracle Valley' when we're in Yorkshire. I believe the Hollybush prophecy was being fulfilled as we moved through 2012. Then in September Lee Palmer suggested a UNITE outing to Wembley Arena to a National Day of Prayer and Worship (NDoP). We joined with another group from our area and the UNITE Pillars and supporters headed South to the famous football ground where we saw JJohn, Godfrey Birtill and the man behind the NDoP,

Jonathan Oloyede. A crowd of slightly more than we were used to (25,000!) pursued the theme of Christian unity in praise, prayer, worship and the Word.

I want to briefly mention the next few UNITE events leading up to January 2013 because, although they had gained momentum locally, the new year saw a significant increase in their popularity and our outreach in other parts of the North of England.

Our good friend, Cliff Roberts managed to procure the hall at Bucknall Methodist Church for our September UNITE event. Again, not the church but the hall! We invited Lee and Lydia Palmer to share their testimony in an interview situation with Cliff. By this time we had gathered round us some fervent local Christians to support us in the outreach of UNITE. We called them 'PILLARS' because they were to help us hold up a 'platform' where the Lord Jesus was to take centre stage. This was as a result of a vision I had of a platform coming down from heaven which the Lord asked us to hold up. He didn't require any special skills from me (just as well!), all He wanted was obedience in putting on that platform at our meetings. This took a lot of stress away from me! By now you will be familiar with the names of some of these 'Pillars'. They were Jean and me, Cliff and Lottie Roberts, Ann Grainger, Lee and Lydia Palmer and Joan Adams. Joan is a good friend from our own church who has supported us and helped Jean so much with food/refreshments.

We tried another interview situation at Bucknall. This was the first time, outside of St John's, that Steve Collier, together with his wife, Michelle plus son Mark and daughter Jess had led worship for us. They were the worship team at St John's then. For some time they were our regular band for all UNITE events. They were brilliant and very talented. They lit up the room with real spiritual fervour! On this occasion it was Cliff interviewing Lee and Lydia. A familiar number of around 80 folks came along to the event although a few 'regulars' were missing. I noted that they were replaced by a group of about six ladies from Tunstall Methodist Church. I thought this was a little unusual. I thought it even more unusual when one of these ladies stood up during the interview and prophesied over the lives of Lee and Lydia. This was our first encounter with Barbara Payne. True to form, Barbara led a young lady to faith in Jesus at the end of the evening.

The next three events are to conclude this chapter as they led up to a new season for the UNITE team. The 'Pillars' remained very close and we would meet together in each other's homes to discuss tactics. Actually our aim was simple. It was the UNITE slogan 'Connecting and Encouraging Christians; Introducing people to Jesus'. We wanted to lift up the name of Jesus, get Christians together and raise a sense of urgency among believers and non-believers that His return to planet earth was something we all needed to be ready for! Or put another way: Plan ahead – It wasn't raining when Noah built the ark!

October through to January saw UNITE events in Tunstall Methodist Church Hall, St James's Church, Newchapel and Hanley Baptist Church. We were so grateful to Rev'd Kim Kerchal, Rev'd Will Slater and Pastor Trevor Nicklin respectively for allowing us to put our events on in their churches: Methodist, Anglican and Baptist! In Tunstall our friend and speaker for the evening, Andrew James, reminded us of a prophetic passage from the scriptures which had been spoken out by Lee Plummer at our meeting in Scholar Green Village Hall six months previously. This was Ephesians 3 verse 20: *'Now to him who is able to do immeasurably more than all we ask or imagine, according to his power that is at work within us, to him be glory in the church and in Christ Jesus throughout all generations, for ever and ever! Amen.'* We had known Andrew very well for several years. He led the house group Jean and I were part of. We also knew that he had been very ill for over twelve months. He had been rushed into hospital on multiple occasions with symptoms of complete disorientation, fitting and considerable pain. His wife Gail and their daughters Francesca and Deborah were so concerned for him. An operation was due where the surgeon would have to cut through Andrew's throat to get to the nerve and tissues at the base of his skull. This operation kept being postponed. I and the other members of the house group had prayed for Andrew a number of times. As a member of our own church he had been prayed for there and his condition had remained the same. It got to the stage that when an appeal went out in our church for folks to go to the front for prayer, Andrew really had little inclination to do so anymore. But he had somehow held on to this scripture from Ephesians from back in April's UNITE event and on 15th July in this year of 2012 during Biddulph Pentecostal Church's Sunday morning meeting an appeal for healing went out. The appeal was given by our friend from Ghana who was staying with Jean and I at the time; Bishop James Kotey. Andrew responded by slowly walking from the back of the church believing God to do immeasurably more than he could ask or imagine. Jean and I watched him proceed to the front. At 6' 4" he was perhaps the tallest man in the church. Bishop James is 5' 5" tall. We really felt the presence of the Holy Spirit at this point and instead of keeping my head bowed and my eyes closed I watched in anticipation. As Bishop James raised his hand over Andrew and commanded healing I watched as the big man fell backwards to the floor and lay there for a few minutes. After this he got to his feet. He was totally healed! Right time, right place, right person. That's the Holy Spirit!

Andrew said that was the first time he had been able to lie completely flat with his head on the floor. His daughters said he was an inch taller than they remembered him over the last twelve months. Something had happened in his neck or skull which couldn't be explained by medical science. He had over thirty items of medication to take daily. By an oversight, Andrew didn't take his medication the following day. But he discovered he didn't need to. This was a permanent healing he could now testify to in this Tunstall UNITE event six months later. Now, in 2020 Andrew is healthy and he stands today as testimony to the healing power procured for us by Jesus' suffering and death on the cross of Calvary almost 2000 years ago. It is still as effective as ever and Andrew will tell you so. And no; Andrew's doctors couldn't explain why he had been healed without an operation.

I recorded the following few sentences relating to the latter part of the evening: *Cliff Roberts and Pastor Trevor Weaver led a rendering of 'There is a Green Hill Far Away' to the tune of 'The House of the Rising Sun'!! Everyone joined in. We had a great meeting! We prayed for St Johns fellowship as Halloween approaches once again, Tunstall Methodist for more of God and breakthrough in their fellowship and for John Tildesley of Tunstall Methodist (our key-holder for the premises) who had been taken into hospital that day.* Although God's healing for Andrew was very remarkable, it should not be considered an isolated event as we will discover in Chapter 4 when three young men testify to miraculous and unexpected healing of serious disease and injury to the head.

To complete this 'season' we decided to hold a UNITE event in our local. I mean in a church which is just up the road from where Jean and I live! This is St James', 'The Church on the Hill' in Newchapel. This was on the invitation of the Curate, Lee Plummer who had spoken in the April event in Scholar Green. We were able to share with him the powerful effect his speaking out that scripture and how Andrew James took it as his motivation to go for prayer. It's a little out-of-the-way for most Potteries folk, but around 65 came to the meeting on a cold, frosty night to hear our speakers Richard Walley and Emma Weaver. People were brought along to the event to be prayed for, and many were. Christmas came and went and on 12th January, 2013 we met in Hanley Baptist Church. This is a church within a short distance of Hanley (known to some as the City Centre!). It has a massive outreach to the homeless and needy. I noticed that there was a 'buzz' in the place (it's not far from the bus station for those of you who speak the dialect!). There were a lot of enthusiastic and excited people gathering well in advance for the meeting which was to begin at 7pm. Steve Collier was setting the mood for the meeting with some anointed praise songs. I can't thank Steve enough for his dedication, commitment and enthusiasm in supporting our events. We always have a time of prayer away from the meeting with a group of those who want to join us in committing the evening to the Lord in prayer. We went into a nearby room to pray at around 6.45pm. The building was looking pretty full at this time. However, when we came out of the prayer room and entered the main church, it was heaving with folks. Someone said they had counted 150 people! I'm not sure there were as many as this, but it demonstrated a quantum leap in support for our event. Steve struck up the chorus '*I went to the enemy's camp and I took back what he stole from me!*' This lit the place up. People wanted what Jesus would give them – victory over the works of the enemy, Satan. Broken people coming to the Lord Jesus in faith, knowing that they had been robbed but that they had been given the authority in prayer to take back what had been stolen from them; their health, their dignity, their family. With all their hearts, these people were praising Jesus, the One they knew made this exchange possible on the cross at Calvary. Hallelujah! To round off this chapter I will simply add what I recorded after the meeting had ended: *'Gerald and Hazel Gleaves gave what they called 'warm-up' testimonies and from that point on the people were on fire! Percy Johnson – originally from Zambia – was our guest for the evening and he gave his testimony of how he was involved in witchcraft to the extent that he was required by the witch-doctor to sacrifice his son. The prayers and pleas of Percy's wife (a Christian lady) brought him to church and he eventually gave his life to Jesus. Percy testified to the reality of spiritual power – of the devil then of the far greater power of God. A good friend of ours responded by testifying that her daughter-in-law had recently joined a witches coven in this country. She told us of the tragedy of the loss of her son through suicide a few months afterwards. We always ask people to use the tea/coffee/ biscuits/cake interval as a time to get to know one another, to link up and to pray for each other. There was much prayer during the interval. Following this, we had testimony after testimony from the floor. So many wanted to share the wonderful things Jesus had done in their lives. We had to wind the meeting up at around 9-45pm and even after that many were still being prayed for. We are very grateful to Pastor Trevor Nicklin who did so much to support and encourage us on the night.*

So that was our early journey. Our first season tasting that the Lord is good. We will now move on to the next season when we 'spread our wings' and put on the UNITE events in other counties in the North of England. We also meet some unusual Christian brothers and sisters.

CHAPTER 3

SPREADING OUR WINGS

*"But you will receive power when the Holy Spirit comes upon you.
And you will be my witnesses, telling people about me
everywhere – in Jerusalem, throughout Judea, in Samaria,
and to the ends of the earth."*
Acts 1:8

In the last chapter we began the early part of our journey which took us to a coffee lounge, a community centre, a television studio dining room, church halls and a number of churches. All these were in North Staffordshire with the 'slight exception' of Scholar Green Village Hall which is just over the border in Cheshire. We had also been quite adventurous with our speakers bringing in John Holme from London and Jean Lupton from Nottingham. But this next season of 'Connecting and encouraging Christians and introducing people to Jesus' was about to take UNITE into Lancashire and Cheshire and introduce local folks to some names which are well known now, but in 2013, were at the beginning of their ministries.

For a few years Jean and I had joined friends, Peter and Shirley Hulme, at their annual conference at the Glendower Hotel in Lytham St Anne's, Lancashire. A good crowd from Stoke-on-Trent would attend to hear a speaker and generally have a good weekend of teaching and fellowship. Throughout 2012 Peter had been suffering with cancer and its treatment and he and Shirley had also lost two close family members. They didn't feel able to run the event in January 2013. In fact, they decided to discontinue these annual conferences which they had faithfully and diligently led for many years. Jean and I picked up on this, and after liaising with Peter and Shirley and discovering that quite a few 'Stokies' would still book into the hotel for a weekend break, we thought maybe we could put on a UNITE weekend in its place. Yes! We decided to go for it! The weekend in question included Saturday 19th January. However as late as a few days before this we had no worship band, no equipment, no speaker and no room available in which to hold a meeting! So on the Thursday we just turned up at the hotel and asked God to help us! We were given a smaller room, 'The Lowther Suite' which cost us nothing, the hotel staff were very good to us. Somehow we'd been put in touch with a lady called Ann Strickland, the pastor of 'Renovate Church' in St Anne's. We didn't know her, but she sent along two really helpful and friendly men from her church, Dave and Brian who came to the hotel to meet me on the Friday evening. They offered to provide keyboard, guitar and vocal support to our praise and worship. I was thrilled and so appreciated their help. God was being good to us!

Heavy snow had fallen in Stoke-on-Trent so that Cliff and Lottie plus a number of others couldn't make the journey on Friday as planned. Apparently Burslem was 'cut off'! However, Cliff and Lottie drove up on the Saturday morning. Others also began to arrive. We were so pleased to see them as our gathering at that time was looking to be pretty small! On the Saturday evening we all had early meals in the restaurant and made our way to the 'Lowther Room' where Dave and Brian had set up and their Christian songs were being noticed by other residents in the hotel. We began with a prayer from Peter Hulme which was fitting and really made it feel as though we were carrying on the Christian witness there in the hotel. At the beginning of the meeting we counted about 23 people present. It was a relatively small room and it suited the number present. Suddenly, there was the sound of a commotion outside the room. Was it a wild party going on in the hotel, or some 'gate-crashers' coming to disrupt the meeting? Next, some glamorous ladies and a few men walked into the room. I said to them "Are you going to a party?" But this was Ann Strickland and some of her folks from the 'Renovate Church' in St Anne's! I like to run a joyful meeting – the joy of the Lord is our strength! But this group of around a dozen brought joy on joy with their encouragement and enthusiasm for the Lord Jesus. I didn't need to ask people to give their testimonies, they just got up and did it. There were some heart-rending stories from both Stoke-on-Trent and St Anne's Christians. Also there was prophecy over a number folks present and a recommitment to follow Jesus from one young man. Dave and Brian did us proud with some really lively praise songs as they led worship. We had 35 in the room and it was full! I have come to realise that God doesn't stop at the end of the UNITE meeting. So many times he has blessed us the following day. Sunday morning was no exception. All the Stoke-on-Trent contingent crowded into 'Renovate Church' in St Anne's to join their morning worship. God was in this. Everyone from very young to old took part. What a weekend!

It was around this early part of the year that I began receiving 'anonymous' texts. 'God bless you bro', 'How are you doing today?', 'It's a blessing to get in touch' and 'Jesus loves you'. I politely answered these for a few weeks until I replied 'But who are you?' I discovered that it was a man who had been given my number by our good friends Bernard and Doreen Adams. They were loyal supporters of UNITE and Doreen had previously testified to her healing almost 12 months before in the Cornerstone Community Centre UNITE event. So I knew the man would be trustworthy. It turned out that the man was texting me from prison! His name was Simon Edwards. As it happens, on his release in July of this year, 2013, Simon was our main speaker at a UNITE event in Stoke-on-Trent. But read about that later in this chapter!

A few weeks later, back in Stoke-on-Trent, we were given Wesley Hall for our Saturday evening event. We had met with Doctor Tom O'Brien a few months previously and arranged for him to speak at the meeting. We put out 100 chairs, underestimating the likely interest in him. By around 6.45pm we found ourselves having to find extra chairs and place them in the corridors beside the hall with the doors open! People just flooded in, some local, some from Middlewich and some from Wigan swelling the attendance to around 140 folks. Tom gave a great testimony of his being born-again. Many others testified. One of these was Melanie Price. The story of her life was amazing, including the years she spent as a fortune-teller on Blackpool pier! But you will have to wait a little to discover more about this. She was to be our speaker three months later in Swan Bank, Burslem.

Before the Swan Bank event, though, we held UNITE meetings in Macclesfield (reaching out into Cheshire), later in February, Longton in March, then Hanley in April, 2013. When we began these events I genuinely thought that we would run out of speakers and venues but now it seemed that churches wanted us and we didn't have enough time to put on all the events!

We'd had a taste of holding UNITE outside our area and I felt that 'spreading our wings' was a good thing. Holding the event in Macclesfield turned out to be quite easy. We had so much help from Pastor Chris Davies of Calvary Christian Centre who did us proud on the night. Although I'd lived in Macclesfield as a boy, I had no idea where the churches were or who was likely to come along to the event. In fact, if I'd walked down the road outside the church I think I would have got lost! This made me think of a quip some wag once made about Billy Graham:

Reverend Billy Graham tells of a time early in his ministry when he arrived in a small town to preach a sermon. Wanting to post a letter, he asked a young boy where the post office was. When the boy had told him, Dr. Graham thanked him and said, "If you'll come to the Baptist Church this evening, you can hear me telling everyone how to get to heaven." The boy replied, "I don't think I'll be there. . . You don't even know your way to the post office."

It wasn't just the geography of the venue, but this 'away-from-home' event had a different flavour about it too. Pastor Chris had organised a Lancashire hotpot for everyone with our guests sitting at tables in their beautiful new building! Free of charge! Around 100 folks arrived for the meeting; I discovered we had Christians from all the Macclesfield churches including the Roman Catholic Church. This was so encouraging; born-again believers coming together to celebrate this wonderful unity which God has gifted to His Church. I found it hard work trying to get people up to testify. Stoke folks were used to it; Macclesfield folks were not. But it did happen and a number got up and testified to what Jesus had done in their lives. Many people were prayed for during the interval before our guest speaker, Peter Gladwin took the floor. The following is an extract from an article I sent to a local newspaper:

'This was Peter Gladwin, who was almost burned to death as a toddler. He survived, but was left with horrific scarring and disabilities. He told how his life followed a course of disastrous

events including criminal activity, gambling, drugs and alcohol addiction. On three occasions he faced death – in a gang fight when he was stabbed, in a hit and run accident and finally at age 29, following his father's suicide, Peter decided he'd had enough and would "end it all." At this point, Peter was to discover that God had a plan for his life. His sister, who unbeknown to him, had only weeks before become a born-again Christian, prayed for him over the phone. Peter gladly accepted Jesus as his Lord and Saviour and his life was dramatically transformed from then on. He later worked for the Probation Service before becoming a full-time evangelist and taking his story all over the UK.'

As I mentioned earlier, God had a way of continuing the Saturday evening blessings into the following day. The final sentence of the newspaper article read: *'Peter visited Styal Prison in Wilmslow the following morning when 18 women committed their lives to Jesus.'*

This has happened time and time again. In fact, if you can manage to read on through to the next chapter you will find a remarkable repeat of this on another occasion when Peter spoke for us in Derbyshire. I forgot to mention; it was not until the next day that I discovered a six year old girl had gone to Peter at the end of the evening to say that she had accepted Jesus into her life as Lord and Saviour! Hallelujah!

Following the Macclesfield event, we met in Longton Elim Church in March with Dave Price as our speaker and then in Hanley Baptist Church in April when Peter Gladwin spoke for us again. Peter was ceaselessly active in the UK at this time and his testimony was compelling. Around 100 came along to each of these events, Steve Collier and family provided music and a number claimed healing following prayer.

If it looks as though lady speakers have been in the minority so far, please continue reading. Our next three UNITE events which took place in May and June exclusively feature lady speakers!

The May event was held in the main church at Swan Bank, Burslem. The coffee lounge where we had met in 2011 would not have held the 100 plus who came to worship God, give testimony and hear Melanie Price's amazing testimony. This was a very lively evening, being described at the time as 'the most powerful meeting we'd had'. 'Golden Voices' from our friend, Marcus Chilaka's RCCG Church (Nigerian background) thrilled us and created a truly yet dynamic worshipful atmosphere with song and dance. This is what I recorded at the time:

Melanie Price spoke of her start in life from a mixed Jewish and Muslim background before marriage at 14 years of age into a travelling community. She became a gypsy fortune-teller on Blackpool Pier. Learning quickly to steal, lie and manipulate, Melanie told us that this all stopped when she had an encounter with Jesus which changed her life. She gave her life to Jesus and was 'born-again' of the Spirit of God. She was totally transformed. She has since travelled the world speaking about the life-changing power of Jesus in over 42 countries. Several others gave their own accounts of how Jesus has changed their lives. At the end of the meeting Melanie prayed individually for around thirty folks – for up to 3-4 minutes each with such great empathy and spiritual insight. Two 8 yr old girls, children from St Johns church – gave their lives to Jesus during the evening. One young woman who came out for prayer, when Melanie began to minister to her, began to scream (loud and prolonged) as an unclean spirit came out of her. After prayer she was peaceful and smiling. At 10pm the Swan Bank keyholder returned to switch off the sound and lock up the building. At this time prayer and ministry was in full swing! At around 10.40pm while Melanie was still praying for people at the front of the church, Ezinne, the leader of the singing group said to me that she felt led by the Holy Spirit to sing a song of praise after praying had finished. I told her that I had such a lot of pressure on me to close the meeting that we would have to forego the praise song. But I felt that if we did not follow this leading, I would be quenching the Holy Spirit. So I went to Ezinne and said "Yes, let's praise Jesus" – so we did! We finished around 11pm!

Our next lady speaker was Julie Brown, a friend of ours from Hollybush Christian Centre in North Yorkshire. You may remember our prophecy there in the introduction to this book. This is an example of how the personal connections we had been making for many years began to blossom in bringing the family of God together. We held the event in Burslem again, this time in St John's Church. Steve Collier was no longer leading worship for us and another 'in-house' group helped us this time. A young lady, Esther Scrimshaw from our own church, sang beautifully for us. Julie was to be one of the speakers later in this month of June at the National 'Transformational Conference' headed by Ed Silvoso in The Bridge Centre in Birches Head. Her quiet testimony proved to be powerful, so deep and passionate about the moving of God's Spirit in our land and in Stoke-on-Trent in particular. Julie prayed for Robinson Asokan, one of the worship band, giving a really encouraging prophetic word of knowledge to Robinson. I have to admit that I failed to move with the way God was leading us on this occasion and I believe I closed the meeting prematurely at 9.50pm. Maybe I was thinking of our May meeting three weeks previously when the keyholder was anxious to get home to watch 'Dr Who'!! However, our friend and Pastor at the church, Lydia, was pleased to have us there as long as it took. As I said before, we built up a really good relationship with all at St John's. But this was a lesson learned for me.

Another lady was our guest speaker at the 29th June UNITE event in 2013 which we held in the Church Hall of Tunstall Methodist Church. She was Raj Jarrett, a former Seikh from Birmingham. Our worship band consisted of a very young group from Hanley Baptist Church ably led by Dan Nicklin. So much went on at this meeting it's impossible to include it all. It would be true to say this about all the meetings; friendships formed, contacts made, people who would never enter a church listening to and responding to the gospel of Jesus Christ. A friend of ours who suffers from agoraphobia (fear of crowds or confined spaces) was persuaded to come to the event. I invited prayer from the floor to begin the meeting. People hesitated, as they usually do at the beginning of the evening, but our 'fearful' friend walked out to the centre of the crowd, took the microphone and began praying. Hallelujah! Holy boldness!

Raj told of her experience of 'honour' violence, abuse of all kinds, forced marriage and attempted murder in her life as a Seikh girl. She related how, at one point, she was being strangled by her partner and as she felt her life slipping away, she cried out to one of the Gods she had heard of – Jesus. Instantly the attacker let her go! She later gave her life to Jesus and vowed to serve Him. For many years her family held a death threat over her. Having given up a well-paid job, she now lives by faith, as does her husband, and she travels the country taking the life-changing message of Jesus to those who live in darkness and abuse, seeing them set free. Her book is well known: 'The Only Arranged Marriage'. In 2015, she was awarded West Midlands Woman of the Year and West Midlands Most Inspirational Woman.

We had a Seikh young man stay for the whole meeting and a Muslim man came in during Raj's talk. It was a powerful message and Lydia and Lee gave the Muslim gentleman their contact details. The following day he phoned them to ask "How do I become a Christian?"

So ended our trilogy of lady speakers, but there were many more to follow.

We had just returned from a holiday in one of our favourite haunts. This was Little Haven in Pembrokeshire. The scenery is stunning, the village is beautiful and Jean and I have spent many happy times there. One evening, as we sat on 'The Point' ('Pentir' in Welsh!) watching the sun going down over the Celtic Sea's horizon, I received a phone call. It was a man called Tyrone Singh. He was phoning from Bedfordshire about an enquiry I'd made to invite an unknown young man to speak at one of our September UNITE meetings. I'm not sure where I had heard about this young man whose name was Daniel Chand, but I felt like 'sticking my neck out' and inviting him anyway. He'd been a Christian for less than a year, he was from an Asian background and he had been in trouble with the Police narrowly escaping prison not long before his conversion. But from what I had seen, he was a born-again believer in the Lord Jesus Christ and he was 'on fire'! This is what UNITE is all about; 'CONNECTING and ENCOURAGING Christians; INTRODUCING people to Jesus'. Anyway, we booked Daniel for our late September event while on holiday in Wales!

In the meantime, in the run-up to this much anticipated UNITE event with Daniel Chand, we called our friend, Trevor Weaver, the Pastor of Bucknall Pentecostal Church and booked in for our July event. It would be something of a special time, firstly because we decided to hold a barbeque before the meeting, secondly because Simon Edwards, fresh out of prison, was to be our guest speaker, and thirdly it was 2013 and I had just celebrated my 65th birthday and had officially become a pensioner! You will recall I mentioned Simon earlier and how we had got to know each other. CONNECTIONS!

Around 100 came to the barbeque, many for the first time. There were ex-prisoners and prison workers together with many core supporters of UNITE enjoying the barbeque in the last of the spell of fine weather we'd had. A thunderstorm was forecast for the afternoon and dark, ominous clouds loomed in the distance. We prayed that the rain would hold off until the end of the barbeque when we agreed it could rain as much as it liked! Cliff and Lottie Roberts excelled with the barbeque in the grounds outside the church. They have always supported us wholeheartedly, and Cliff does a mean burger. Everyone drifted into the church just before 7pm as a few drops of rain began to fall. By the time everyone was seated the few drops had turned into a deluge! Thank you Lord for looking after us! The heavens opened in more ways than one as Trevor led praise and worship in his inimitable and energetic style. This was always going to be a lively meeting with such a diverse gathering of people.

Then Simon came on with his testimony. This was fresh and new and saturated with vision and potential. He spoke about Dovegate Prison where he spent much of his sentence for several armed robberies, and how he met with Jesus there. Simon said that between 2006 and 2009 around 1,000 men genuinely committed their lives to Jesus in that prison, and this included the Assistant Governor, Ray Duckworth! This was an amazing revival and something of which I was totally unaware. Simon's outlook, attitude and position had improved dramatically following his decision to follow Christ; so much so, he was given a position on Prison Reception. This meant that Simon saw men who had genuinely committed their lives to Jesus leave prison with a little over £40 in their pockets. Many had no home, no job and no future to 'walk' out into. Simon then saw them return to prison a short time afterwards because they had no help to turn from their former way of life. Surely this wasn't right. He began to imagine what it would be like for these born-again men to receive contact and encouragement from the community where they would be living before their sentence ended. What would it be like to have a place to live, Christian friends to encourage them, or a job to go to and a church that would accept ex-cons? This became a vision which Simon knows came from God. Earlier in the year Simon and I had met at the gates of Dovegate Prison near Uttoxeter. Because of the many connections Jean and I had made, Simon came with us on a tour of the Stoke-on-Trent churches on several Sundays prior to his release. No we didn't 'spring' him from prison! He was allowed out on licence one day a week and he had to be back by 8.45pm – or else! We did manage to return him on time. This enabled Simon to share his vision with many local churches and to prepare them for an influx of men from backgrounds considerably different from the norm. The ministry was to be called 'WALK'.

It was very early days as Simon spoke at this July barbeque UNITE event, and people present were inspired, enlightened and encouraged to hear his testimony, his vision and plans to serve God in such an innovative way. We couldn't hold back several other ex-prisoners who were thrilled to share their Christian testimonies. Also speaking about this 'Revival' in the prison were Sandy Hicks (Dovegate Prison Chaplain) and Andrea Stafford. Andrea was part of the Chaplaincy team and a Bible Studies Tutor and one-on-one

Christian Counsellor. It can't be emphasised how much the ministry of these ladies has impacted the lives of so many of these men. Much prayer and much prophecy were delivered in the meeting. ENCOURAGEMENT! As the years have passed, it is remarkable to see how God has moved with Simon's vision and to see the progress made in the lives of so many men who have been afforded the opportunity to 'WALK' out of prison into a new life.

I recorded that during this meeting a man from a Muslim background had committed to going to St John's Church to discuss beginning a ministry to Muslims. I believe this was a carry-over from our Tunstall event in June.

It was August again and Jean and I took the opportunity to take a weekend break in our beloved Yorkshire. We had met John Gaughan a few years earlier when he spoke at Hollybush. John was a rock musician in the late sixties and seventies and if you are of a certain age you will recognise some of the bands he was part of: Marmalade, The Hollies, The Fortunes, The Drifters and, notably, Herman's Hermits. John had a marvellous encounter with Jesus Christ and his life was transformed from that of an alcoholic about to commit suicide to a vibrant one of service to the Lord. John is now a pastor with The International Christian Church Network (TICCN). I mention John because he is a Yorkshireman. He always maintained that God is a Yorkshireman. When asked why, he would reply "Because He is always right." (Yorkshiremen always maintain they are right!). This August of 2013 we visited Hollybush and met many Christian friends there. Pastor Jim always gives us an opportunity to share our UNITE adventures!

Summer was turning into Autumn as we headed out to East Staffordshire for our mid-September UNITE event in the United

Reformed Church, Uttoxeter. This is a small market town a good way out of Stoke-on-Trent and I loved the association with Dr Johnson. Perhaps the most famous event to have occurred in Uttoxeter is the penance of Samuel Johnson. Johnson's father ran a bookstall on Uttoxeter market, and young Samuel once refused to help out on the stall. When Johnson was older, he stood in the rain (without a hat) as a penance for his failure to assist his father. This event is commemorated with the Johnson Memorial, which stands in the Market Place in the town centre and there is also an area of town called Johnson Road, which commemorates him. I've said it before, that Dr Johnson was the best friend the Barber family ever had!

Lloyd Cooke was our speaker for the evening and although there were only around 40 present he went down well. His testimony was inspired, and several ministers and pastors were present in addition to some local people. His theme was, 'Are we giving God our full and undivided attention?' It was a word in season for just about all of us.

We now come to the UNITE event I mentioned earlier. The one where I was 'sticking my neck out'! A small team of us went out on the streets of Burslem during the afternoon telling people about Jesus and inviting them to the evening event in St John's Church which was beginning to be a regular UNITE haunt. Please pardon the use of that word in the light of my previous mention of the alleged witch, Molly Lee, whose gravestone is in the churchyard! She is said to haunt the area! All the arrangements came together on the day as a team of young men and women arrived in the car park which looks over onto the disused and overgrown site of Acme Marles pottery works where three neglected bottle kilns known as 'The Three Sisters' still stand. The almost abandoned road opposite the church used to be the main route from town to St John's. It was called Church Street, but in the 1950s it was renamed after my 3xgreat-grandfather's friend and partner in the gospel, Hugh Bourne. The road is now called Bourne's Bank. This is not the most presentable part of our city to introduce our friends from the south. However, once inside the church, though it is rather old-fashioned with pews, there was definitely a buzz of excitement as the building began to fill up. We always take time to pray before the meetings, and when we emerged from the small vestry, the place was heaving! Someone in the balcony counted 140 folks.

The beautiful voice of 16 year old Esther Scrimshaw brought us into the presence of God before our guest speaker took to the front of the church. Against my own policy, I'd never met our speaker before and only seen him on Youtube. What would he be like? Would he be too young, too inexperienced, too brash? He'd only been a Christian a short time. Would the Potteries folks take to him? I needn't have worried about these things. This is what I recorded following the event:

Daniel Chand, just turned 22 and from an Asian family, his life had consisted of boxing, clubbing and drinking and he finally got into trouble with the Police during a night out. Before the case got to Crown Court, Daniel got to know something about the love of Jesus from a friend. He had heard that faith in God could move mountains. He prayed that the 'mountain' of the serious, impending case would be removed. On the day of the hearing, the case simply collapsed. This didn't stop him from going out and getting drunk that night and having to be carried home. However, he told us that the next morning at 5 o'clock he woke up completely sober and felt God's love simply enveloping him. He responded to that love and gave his life fully to Jesus who has used him in the 18 months he has been a Christian to take God's word seriously. His testimony and message were fresh and free from religious talk. He was very popular with everyone. At the end of the evening a number of young folks made decisions to commit their lives to Jesus. INTRODUCING PEOPLE TO JESUS! Several were healed from asthma, arthritis and other ailments. We are still receiving reports of healings having taken place during the event. One of these was Francesca James who had broken both her wrists and was experiencing stiffness and pain. Francesca is the daughter of Andrew who received an amazing healing earlier in the year. This was an awesome Spirit-filled evening!!

So we come to the end of this season of 'spreading our wings' into Lancashire and Cheshire and bringing in speakers from far afield. We also come to the end of this chapter and begin to embark on a new season; soaring on wings like eagles, meeting with some opposition, encountering some weird situations, enjoying every minute and giving God all the glory!

CHAPTER 4

VISION

Where there is no vision, the people perish
Proverbs 29:18

In Chapter 2, I spoke about 'pillars' and a 'platform' in an abstract sort of way meaning our handful of seven original supporters (pillars) and the opportunity (platform) for Christians to share their testimonies. I am rarely given pictorial visions from God, but very early in our UNITE adventures I did have a vision of a 'platform' coming down from heaven. I prayed about this and I felt that the Holy Spirit was telling me that God was giving us a 'platform' upon which Jesus was to take centre-stage at all our meetings. He required the platform to be supported. We were the ones to support the platform. We were the 'pillars'! I was humbled to receive this because it meant that I wouldn't feel under pressure to be someone I wasn't. I mean I didn't have to be 'super-spiritual' or a great leader to press on with these ever-expanding UNITE events. It took a lot of pressure off me. If anyone should think that I, Jean or any of our 'pillars' were more important than the least of any one of the folks who came to the meetings, let me reassure you that we are not. Watching 'Songs of Praise' last evening, a lady in her eighties was being interviewed. She loved the Lord Jesus, but said she didn't feel that she had any special 'gift'. However, in her lifetime she had adopted a boy with special needs and fostered many, many other children. I thought, now there is a special Christian lady with an awesome gift of compassion! I genuinely believe that if any believer is prepared to make themselves available to God, they will be amazed at what He can do with what they have to offer.

In the following season of UNITE events let's become time-travellers! Let us begin in October 2013 and travel through to May 2015; from spreading our wings to soaring like eagles?! The May 2015 event saw a young man who was a Chief Inspector of Police as our speaker. You will be surprised by the content of his testimony. In between, Terry Eckersley featured prominently in several of our meetings, most notably in St Anne's when a LGBT Church turned up! But back to October 2013; we were privileged to find ourselves in Longton Central Hall thanks to the hospitality of Rev'd Jeff Short.

In this quite old-fashioned but very spacious building we had a popular young worship leader in Scott Calvert, we had a group of teenagers from several churches, we had a young lady called Lisa Smith who sang beautifully plus around 100 others who came along. The teenagers had decided among themselves that they wanted to begin a 'Youth UNITE' group so we were very much expecting things to happen among them as the Holy Spirit moved that evening. Peter Gladwin came along to support Terry Eckersley who was our speaker for the evening. Terry testified and invited people to receive what God had for them. We were looking for young people to receive Jesus as they had in the last UNITE event in Burslem. However, God had other ideas, and a lady in her late 60s and not a churchgoer, walked from the back of the church to the altar and gave her life to Jesus. Following this, she began to speak in tongues!! The next day, we had lunch with Peter Gladwin, Terry, and Simon Edwards. Peter said that he had just been to Cwmbran where, in this year of 2013 there had been 'an outpouring of the Holy Spirit' and he'd seen many commit their lives to Jesus and many receive healing. Peter said that he experienced the power of God fall there. However, he said the Holy Spirit fell more powerfully in Central Hall!!!

Our last event before Christmas was held in Penkhull Christian Fellowship when Carl Finnan from United Christian Broadcasters was our guest speaker. At that time Carl was UCB's Youth and Childrens' Outreach director. Co-incidentally a young lady called Sassi Beeri from Hungary joined us and told us about her passion for sharing the gospel with young people. She was the newly-appointed director of 'Youth for Christ'. Remember Sassi as she will figure in a 'God-incidence' in a UNITE meeting early the following year. Carl gave a very moving account of his life and how he accepted Jesus as his Lord and Saviour. This was the occasion on which we first met Anthony Bostock, a former prisoner who gave an extremely 'on fire' testimony. 'Golden Voices' from RCCG were absolutely brilliant leading worship.

Christmas came and went and very soon we found ourselves in January 2014 and at 'Burslem Lighthouse'. No, we were nowhere near the sea; we were in the 'Mother Town' of Stoke-on-Trent once again! This time in the building shared between the United Reformed Church and the Elim Church. However, only one week later we would be back beside the seaside to put on the UNITE event in St Anne's. The Burslem event marked the arrival of Elim's new pastor, Jim Lowe, a gifted and enthusiastic young man who is now our neighbour living only a few doors away from Jean and me. This was the first time for UNITE in this venue and I received phone calls from a number of folks who couldn't find it. Bear in mind it's called 'The Lighthouse'! Over 100 people crowded into the church to hear the amazing testimonies of three young men who had each suffered severe illnesses or potentially fatal injury to their heads.

We had prayed fervently for each of these young men some time previously, both at UNITE meetings and at other fellowship groups we are part of. Although I had called them 'The Three Headcases', you will only remember two of them: Andrew James and 18 year old Tom Buckett. My ambition was to get all three together testifying to God's miracle working power of healing through prayer. This time Tom testified himself and so did Andrew. The only missing 'Headcase' was 19 year old James Adams who was represented by his mum. Briefly, James developed a brain tumour which prevented him taking his 'A' levels. His future was uncertain, but now, seven years on James is a qualified doctor! The power of prayer! If you will travel forward in time with me to May 2017, you will find Dr Adams lighting up Trentham Parish Church at our UNITE event there – Chapter 8. It was a thrill and a privilege to be led in worship by a band from our friends at 'Living Word' Filipino Church.

A few days later Jean and I, together with 'Pillar' Joan Adams and friend Sheila Walton, headed up the M6 towards Blackpool turning left onto the M55 to arrive at the Glendower Hotel in Lytham St Anne's for our second UNITE event there. This time we hired the ballroom and saw around 15 friends from Stoke-on-Trent join with Christians from Lytham, Blackpool and Bolton swelling the number to 50. It was great to see new faces and make connections with Christian brothers and sisters from the Lancashire area. So many new testimonies were shared and friendships made. This encouraged me to try and grow this annual event in St Anne's. As I mentioned earlier, it is not easy to encourage people to come out on a Saturday evening. It's even more difficult when people have to be reached from a distance. I began to put in many hours of work during November and December contacting churches, pastors and contacts, plus getting advertising in the local press and radio. This paid off in future years as the next January UNITE event saw 70 attend. This increased over the years to around 100, mostly folks from the Blackpool area. Once again, 'Renovate Life' Ann Strickland's church provided music to lead us in praise and worship. Unfortunately Ann was suffering with laryngitis. Peter Gladwin gave his testimony in an instructive and appealing way and many recommitted their lives to Jesus at the end of the evening.

We had already held two UNITE events in 2014 before we returned to Bucknall Pentecostal Church where we celebrated our 30th meeting in February. Once again, Simon Edwards came along together with several of the 'lads' from his new and thriving 'WALK' Ministry in Tunstall. Each testified of Jesus' love and liberating power in their lives. Some of these men, newly released from prison, prayed for those with illnesses during the interval. Dave Garner spoke about the significant move of God in St John's in the 1960s as the 'Charismatic Renewal' got underway.

March saw us once again in Silverdale. This time we couldn't use the Community Centre as a Filipino Church had begun to have Saturday meetings in there. Now in 2020 there is also an Indian Church meeting in that building. Pastor Edwin very kindly allowed us to use the main church. A young band from Hanley Baptist Church headed up by Ollie Wilson led us in praise and worship. It was great to see these teenagers being such a strategic part of this UNITE event. Melanie Price was our speaker. She was about to leave for missionary work in Hungary. Here's the co-incidence – Jean likes to call this a 'God-incidence' – Sassi Beeri, originally from Hungary herself, came along to the event and she and Melanie got together. As a result Melanie will now meet Sassi's parents out there and in the meantime was able to encourage her and be a friend. My dauhter Caroline, met with Aimee Scoffins, Julia Morrison and also with Ann Grainger. This was very good for her and I thank God He has given me the ministry of introducing people to each other – for His glory! CONNECTIONS!

It was 29th March, 2014 and the clocks were due to go forward one hour that night! For some time my good friend Pastor Jude Emelifionwu had been asking us to put on a UNITE event in Stafford. Jude and his team had 'planted' an RCCG Church in that town within the premises of Sandon Road Baptist Church building. This was significant in the Kingdom of God. However, I learned a lesson in the promotion of our events. I left the advertising to a contact in Stafford, so on arrival I expected the event to attract around 100 folks. However only 40 turned up. I was a little disappointed because John Holme (remember John from one of our 2012 events – and the Richard and Judy Show!) gave his typically animated, humorous but deadly serious message about the necessity for individuals in our nation to come to know the Lord and how we can be involved in that by simply telling them about Jesus. There were testimonies from three ex-prisoners who live in the Stafford 'WALK' house. These were from the heart and gave us a wonderful revelation of God's love and patience with people who were once in the hands of the devil. If ever I complain that the numbers attending our events are lower than I would have liked, Jean always tells me that God will send along the people He wants to be there. I reply that if God wasn't interested in numbers, why did He write a book of that title?!

April took us to the Methodist Church in Endon. It is a lovely building and it was great to make new connections there. It's also a little out of the way, so I wasn't expecting too many folks to come along. I normally try to make the meetings as accessible as possible especially for those who have to use the buses. I tried to get as many young folks there as I could in order to encourage each other in their Christian faith, but there were a number of Youth Camps on and many were away at that time. However, there were around four teenagers there. The atmosphere was amazing and charged with Holy Spirit presence as we opened the meeting in prayer. One of the Stafford 'WALK' men, Levi, came along and once again gave the testimony our friends in Stafford had heard the month before. Levi related how he had committed his life to Jesus and was so grateful to 'WALK' and to his God for making a new life possible for him. This sort of testimony was new to many of the folks who come to the UNITE events. There were perhaps around 60 folks present, some of whom had never been to a UNITE event before. However, at around 8pm there was some noise from outside followed by a steady flow of young people coming in and filling the church. Around 35 Filipino Christians from the Living Word Church in Longton made their entrance! We were overjoyed! What an encouragement these young teenagers were! After the interval, when several were prayed for, Bob Eaton, our guest, gave his testimony. It was humble, funny and entertaining. It was also relevant to many people's lives and extremely moving as Bob told us of his lack of self-esteem and his unsuccessful suicide attempts following a series of 'failures' in his life. Thanks to Bob's now wife, Jill, he went along to church and then to a Billy Graham Crusade where he committed his life to Jesus. He has since taken the gospel all around the world! A good new link with that Methodist Church in Endon!! The first Facebook comment I saw the next day was: "What a cracking time we had at UNITE on Saturday"

Our friend, Pastor Lydia Palmer suggested we really needed a Stoke-on-Trent Day of Prayer which would focus on certain themes in our city where several problems were evident. The suggestions were 1) young people, 2) schools, 3) unity among the churches under the headship of Jesus, and 4) the occult. The 'Pillars' prayed about this and the Day of Prayer was arranged for 14th July in Hanley Baptist Church. I'd just like to put this in context if I can. In North Staffordshire around this time a spiritualist meeting had been advertised to take place in one of the schools. A brave young Christian lady and Classroom Assistant had gone to the head teacher to oppose this on Christian principles, but to no avail. So she mobilised the churches to pray against the meeting. Many churches got involved to pray against it and although the tickets were virtually sold-out, almost unbelievably, the event was kicked out of the school! But that's not all! Evangelist Peter Gladwin was then allowed into the school to speak in the assembly and to encourage the children. Two months later in July, Peter was the guest of honour at the annual prize-giving when he spoke to around 300 parents and pupils about his Christian faith. We thanked God for this which encapsulated the four prayer points exactly!

In the meantime we were to hold two Saturday evening UNITE events. The May event was held in St Mark's Church, Shelton when a man committed his life to Jesus during the meeting. The June event was in St John's when many were prayed for. The speaker was Ellis Kettle, a prison chaplain with some very down-to-earth stories to tell. Jean and I were a little later than usual arriving at St John's as we were delayed somewhat by a beautiful celebration of the marriage of two friends; Simon Edwards and Karen Morton! Their wedding was on 24th June.

So the 12th July arrived and we began our Day of Prayer at 12noon going through to 7pm to enable as many folks as possible to come along. I spend a lot of time putting out paper posters for all the UNITE events and one gentleman came having seen my poster in

Hanley Market! At one point there were twelve people praying, at other times there were only two, but prayer was continuous throughout the day. Two local vicars joined us as did did Lloyd Cooke, Saltbox Chief Executive, who had spoken for us at our Uttoxeter event the previous September. Pastor Trevor Nicklin of Hanley Baptist Church opened the session. It felt very worthwhile to spend the day in prayer with whoever would come and join us. There is one story I'd like to share about this day. Just after we began, a youngish American man made himself known to me. A former US soldier, he had found himself in the UK in a relationship which had sadly broken up. He was left with no home, no money and no job. In his own words, he was skint! I could see he was not in a very good mood – to put it mildly. His other news was that he had been unable to obtain any of his army pension, and wouldn't be able to for some considerable time. He was desperate! I suggested we pray and he seemed open to that. However, his mobile phone rang a few minutes into our prayer and he simply walked off. Ten minutes later he returned with a completely different expression on his face. He was smiling and excited. Apparently, the phone call was from the U.S. informing him that money was being sent over to him. He said to me "If that's what prayer does, I'm interested!" We were privileged to pray for many. That was the UNITE Day of Prayer for Stoke-on-Trent.

It was now 26th July, 2014. Time for our annual barbeque UNITE event. This time we opted for Tunstall Methodist Church Hall. It was a beautiful day and the large car park lent itself to our outdoor barbeque. Once again, Cliff and Lottie were amazing, feeding around 120 folks with burgers, hot dogs and drinks. Afterwards we all trooped into the church hall where Bishop James Kotey from Ghana spoke and ministered powerfully. Often the response to

James' ministry is that people fall on the floor in what is called being 'slain in the Spirit'; this was no exception. Many were prayed for. Unexpected guests who enjoyed James' ministry were Pastor Jude Emelieonwu and Pastor 'Taps' Mtemachani, plus our American friend whom we'd met at our Day of Prayer. He didn't know what to make of these unusual happenings! He was still 'searching' and we continued praying for him. Keep reading to find out more!

In the meantime we arranged to hold an event in Derbyshire in August. Our friend, Evangelist Terry Eckersley, invited us to hold this first in the Genesis Centre, Alfreton. However at a later stage we had to switch to the older but beautiful, stately Alfreton Hall. It is always difficult to attract people to an event they know nothing about, and the Alfreton folks had never heard of UNITE. I really felt that perhaps it was a mistake to put this event on and Jean and I travelled over to Alfreton to tell Terry that we would rather not do it. But Terry was indefatigable – that's a good word to describe Terry! Of course, he persuaded us it would be OK, he would get over 100 folks to come along. So we gave in and decided to go ahead. Peter Gladwin was to be our speaker. I circulated all the local churches with letters and emails, sent out many posters and advertised the event on Facebook. Press releases were sent to local newspapers and radio stations to advertise the event. BBC Radio Derby broadcast an interview with Peter.

Saturday 16th August arrived. It was a pleasant evening and Jean and I had driven out into darkest Alfreton which is almost on the Nottinghamshire border. Together with our friend and 'Pillar', Joan Adams, we booked into our B&B, Chrich Lane Farm in Wessington just outside Alfreton. We also booked in Peter Gladwin who was to stay the night with us. Everything was going according to plan. We took the short drive over to Alfreton Hall where we met with

Terry and his wife, Jill. Our worship leader was getting the sound system sorted, the caretaker of the hall was going to stay with us for the duration of the meeting and we looked forward to the 100 or so folks who were going to turn up. Following our prayer meeting, 7pm approached and only one or two folks had arrived. This was a new experience! What was the obvious thing to do next? I went outside and prayed "Lord, please send some people along to this meeting, and be glorified in Jesus' name. Amen" Well, a few more did arrive. When I say a few, I mean we had eight people attend. Counting the caretaker, worship leader, Terry, Jill, Peter, Joan, Jean and me, our meeting consisted of sixteen people. To say I was disappointed was an understatement! But Jean reminded me that God has the people there He wants to be there. I went along with that!

We had some great praise and worship, some inspired prayer, a number of remarkable testimonies came from people in the gathering and this was followed by the most amazing testimony and ministry of Peter Gladwin. Two young people gave their lives to Jesus for the first time. One of these was the caretaker who was led in a prayer of salvation during the interval. One young woman renewed her commitment to the Lord and another young lady was seriously delivered from unclean spirits. The lady was very disturbed before this deliverance which was carried out in a separate room to the meeting. This was done according to Jesus' instruction in Mark 16:17, *"And these signs will accompany those who believe: in my name they will drive out demons. . ."* This lady is now a mature Christian and is going on with her walk with the Lord. I was overwhelmed. What a night!

However, the Lord hadn't finished with us yet, and once more we were to witness the blessing of the evening carried over to the next day.

Peter, Joan Adams, Jean and I returned to our local B&B at Chrich Lane Farm just outside Alfreton where we spent the night. The following morning, following a superb breakfast, we headed back to Stoke-on-Trent. We all intended to go to the 'Potter's House' in Birches Head to worship (they put on a later service at 11.15am). Again, God had other plans. After taking a wrong turn and passing through a little village, Jean, Joan and I spotted a church with a number of people standing outside. Nothing unusual about that – it was Sunday morning. But for some reason we all said together "Why don't we go there?" Peter, who was following in his car flashed his lights and we stopped. I walked back to him and said "What's up?" He replied "Let's go to that church!" So we did. None of us had any idea where we were nor what church this was, and, being a man, I wasn't going to ask directions! I didn't have a clue where we were! We later discovered it was Watchorn Methodist Church.

As soon as we entered we felt so welcome and full of anticipation of what God was going to do. There was a baby (Called Reuben) who was going to be dedicated by the lovely minister, Rev'd John Peters. Before we realised what was happening, Peter Gladwin was given the opportunity to speak instead of the scheduled preacher. This is not something which usually happens! Peter spoke, and five people, most of them young, made commitments of their lives to Jesus for the first time!! Hallelujah! The large congregation sang the hearty Methodist hymn, 'And can it be' to close the service. But it didn't end there. Following the hymn, The Minister went over to Peter and said, "Peter, there are more people in here who need to give their lives to Jesus. Will you give another appeal?" So Peter did just that, and guess what! Two more young people made first time commitments to Jesus. Another rather interesting detail was that the family with many guests who had come to have their baby christened, had come a week too soon. There had been a mix up with the dates I later discovered. God moves in mysterious ways His wonders to perform!

I should mention that this particular Sunday was Jean's birthday. What a beautiful birthday surprise! We made many contacts in that beautiful church!! My vision of God's platform with Jesus taking centre-stage was becoming reality. I was learning that God does not work only in certain places where acceptable styles of worship, doctrines or denominations are in place, but where the gospel of Jesus Christ is proclaimed in the confident belief that God will honour His promise to needy souls. For *"whoever calls on the name of the Lord shall be saved." How then shall they call on Him in whom they have not believed? And how shall they believe in Him of whom they have not heard? And how shall they hear without a preacher? And how shall they preach unless they are sent?* (Romans 10:13-14) In sending Peter Gladwin to that church, God fulfilled this scripture.

Before we move on to our much-anticipated second UNITE event with Daniel Chand, here's a lesson I learned while driving through the Derbyshire countryside: Moses was leading his people through the desert for 40 years. It seems, even in Biblical times men avoided asking the way!

Now is an opportunity to pause and reflect on past events and look forward to what God had in mind for the remainder of this 'season'. The expression 'SELAH' is used in the Bible 74 times, mostly in the Book of Psalms. Its meaning is interpreted in a number of different ways, but we'll take 'intermission' for our purposes here.

SELAH

CHAPTER 5

BRIGHTER VISIONS BEAM AFAR

Sages leave your contemplations; Brighter visions beam afar;
Seek the great Desire of nations; Ye have seen His natal star.
James Montgomery

Many of those who have been to the UNITE meetings will know that I like to keep things moving with some light-hearted banter; even the odd song or two. When Daniel Chand came to Hanley Baptist Church in September 2014 we had a bumper crowd of around 130; many friends came from around the country to support him. From Liverpool, Andy Cannon and his wife Jen came along. We got on well and Andy began to feature in many of our future events, notably our 100th. As Daniel had been quite an accomplished boxer before he was saved, I jokingly asked him if he had remembered to bring his boxing gloves with him so that he and I could entertain the folks there with an exhibition boxing match. He had to reply that he hadn't. I was teasing him, but that didn't put him off as he brought his fresh and moving testimony of how God had totally transformed his life. Daniel is very strong on the power of the blood of Jesus shed for us sinners on the cross of Calvary, the presence and power of the Holy Spirit to save and heal and the importance of knowing who Jesus is and putting our trust in Him. His ministry that night was radical and effective – I recorded the feedback from our friend, Ismael Mendoza, an Elder at the Philippines-based 'Living Word' Church. He put it like this: *"God was truly present at Unite this evening – we witnessed supernatural miracles including healings, receiving the gift of tongues and people accepting Jesus Christ as their Lord and saviour! Praise, glory and honour to Christ alone!"*

Jean and I were so surprised and rather upset to see some adverse comments about Daniel on Facebook the following day. But five pastors present, some of them quite conservative, were very much supportive of Daniel's message. We learned that we couldn't please everyone and that sometimes there will be criticism. It was a meeting which people still speak about now. Jean and I were very pleased with the evening. We were even more pleased when Daniel and Tanya invited us to their wedding which was to take place later in the year!

A week later on 4th October, 2014, we held our 40th UNITE event in the New Life Centre in Cheadle (Staffs). It was a rather last-minute opportunity to meet and host a wonderful Christian lady who happened to be in our area at the time. Bill Partington, at that time was Head of Strategic Ministry Relations at Stoke-on-Trent based United Christian Broadcasters – the UK's largest Christian media organisation. Bill introduced Jean and I to Fiona Castle. Fiona is the widow of the famous musician and entertainer, Roy Castle – dancer, singer, comedian, actor, television presenter, musician and CHRISTIAN! She spoke beautifully at our event, and we often remark on one of the things she said. "Over every church exit there should be a sign saying 'Servant's Entrance'"! An unfortunate thing which I remember about the evening was the start of a cough which plagued me for over seven months! Some wag told this joke:

The doctor said to the patient: "Your coughing sounds much better."
The patient replies: "No wonder. I've spent a lot of time practising."

The second event we held in October 2014, was in Congleton, Cheshire, outside Stoke-on-Trent, but only just. Our home in Packmoor is only seven miles away from the New Life Church where Terry Eckersley was to be our speaker. In addition to Terry, Martin Hawke from 'Compassion' gave a presentation for that excellent Christian charity which encourages sponsorship for children in poorer parts of the world. One coincidence here was that Terry Eckersley is also a 'Compassion UK Ambassador'. Another coincidence was that as Martin spoke, he testified about a man who had counselled him over the phone ten years earlier at a particularly low point in his life. As it happened, that man was present in our meeting! They had never met and the man in question had only recently moved to Cheshire from the south of England. The name of the man was David Green. David and his wife, Jan, are co-founders of 'Christian TV' and have helped us at UNITE several times. We were so grateful to have met them on this night, and so was Martin! So that was two coincidences. Before Terry spoke, our friend and 'Pillar', Joan Adams, who had travelled with us to the event, felt that the Lord had given her a message about an 'open door'. Terry's message was 'Beyond the Open Door is a fresh and new anointing'!! Actually, there were more coincidences than this but we'll settle for three of what Jean calls 'God-incidences'. Around 30 folks were ministered to in prayer by Terry at the end of the meeting.

The clocks were put back an hour that night and we all had an extra hour's sleep. A few weeks later Jean and I made our way down to Bedford where we had booked into the Mercure Bedford Centre Hotel. As 'strangers and pilgrims in this world' I would have liked us to have stayed in the Pilgrim's Progress hotel (Bedford is renowned as the home of John Bunyan, the writer of 'Pilgrim's Progress')!

If you remember, Daniel and Tanya had invited us to their wedding which was to take place on 15th November. We decided to stay the Friday night in the hotel as that was the venue for the reception later the following day. On the Saturday we had planned to travel down to London for the wedding ceremony then return to the hotel. As we drove down the M1 I noticed the temperature gauge on our oldish Mitsubishi was beginning to rise to new heights! The engine was definitely overheating as we passed Northampton. I took it steady and we arrived safely in Bedford. But how were we going to get to London the next day? The breakdown service arrived and couldn't repair the radiator but recommended 'Radweld' a fluid to make a temporary repair. We didn't trust that; we felt helpless! I received a phone call from Andy Cannon at around 1am to say they were travelling down from Liverpool to stay in the same hotel. Andy offered to take us to London. Problem solved!

Actually what happened was that a large double-decker bus had been chartered to take lots of wedding guests from Bedford to London the next day. We had to rise early on Saturday morning to catch the bus so I had little sleep. I'm one of those folks who need lots of sleep but never manage to get enough! I was suffering badly with my cough which had begun the evening of the Fiona Castle UNITE event. We were grateful to Andy and his wife, Jen, who drove us to Daniel's parent's house where we assembled to catch the bus for our 50 mile journey to London. We thought we'd arrived in the 'nick of time' and that the bus needed to depart so as to arrive in London on schedule. We reckoned without the gracious hospitality of Daniel's family; parents, brother, uncles, aunts, cousins and many friends who were there to help with the preparations. This was real Indian hospitality and hurry wasn't on the agenda. The tea was brewed for a very long time to achieve perfection, but eventually we set off, arriving at Pinner Baptist Church on time! On the way, the ladies wearing saris were singing Christian songs in Bengali. They asked me to sing them in English for some of the others to join in. So I did! I I loved it, despite my cough!

We were thrilled to be part of the wedding and the reception later. Around 350 people celebrated in very loud and lively Indian-style. A beautiful marriage of two beautiful people. The following day Jean and I limped home up the M1 having used the 'Radweld'!

At the end of November we held our last UNITE event of 2014. Bill Partington, who had recently introduced us to Fiona Castle, was speaking and giving his testimony on this evening in Bucknall Pentecostal Church. He shared how his life had been impacted by God from an early age through a variety of circumstances including a near-fatal car crash. Bill was a policeman for a while and he recalled telling a tramp to turn out his pockets. The tramp, who had nothing, replied "You're a hard man." This affected Bill – a Holy Spirit discipline lesson! At the end, there was some very worthwhile prayer ministry.

Christmas 2014 came and went. We had snow in December; I checked the photos stored on my laptop. Jean and I enjoyed the picturesque winter landscape around Knypersley Pool, our local beauty spot. Unfortunately it wasn't a white Christmas! However, through December I was preparing for two firsts; our first UNITE event in 2015 and our first one in Biddulph (the town of our own church). I wasn't too sure that we would be able to attract too many locals; a prophet being without honour in his own town! Amy Wyatt, the pastor of the Oasis Community Church just outside the town had been one of my main encouragers to put this meeting on in Biddulph, but it turned out that she had arranged to have her baby, Jack, dedicated on the same afternoon. In addition to this, Biddulph is a bit out of the way. I wasn't sure what to expect after hiring the spacious Town Hall.

Saturday evening, 10th January arrived and a few 'Pillars' plus others joined together to pray for the meeting. We prayed in the kitchen at around 6.45pm. By 7pm we returned to the main hall and it was packed! People came from everywhere as well as many locals, and I think this was the first time our very good friends, Malc and Steph Grey-Smart from Market Drayton, came to a UNITE meeting. What a contrast to our August event in Alfreton Hall! Simon Edwards spoke, Paul Critchley led worship and our Filipino friends from 'Living Word' Church brought their young girls along and they performed a beautiful dance to an inspiring Christian song. A good number of men from WALK, all ex-prisoners, came with Simon. There was considerable ministry and prayer for people at the end of the evening and Melanie Price was invaluable in helping us with this.

A few days later, together with our friends Joan and Sheila, we headed up the M6 towards Lytham St Anne's for our third event in the Glendower Hotel. I had been working hard through November and December to muster support for the event in the Blackpool/St Anne's area. This time, Ann Strickland and our friends from the 'Renovate' Church couldn't be with us and we met a man who was to become a good friend and great encourager of UNITE. This was Pastor Steve Moss, and his worship group came along and helped us no end. They were lively and fervent and led worship brilliantly. Around 70 came to the hotel ballroom from the different churches locally adding to the increasing group who had travelled from Stoke-on-Trent. I really loved this coming together in one accord. This, and our shared love of Jesus was what UNITE is all about.

There was an atmosphere of expectancy. Terry Eckersley was our speaker and in his characteristic forthright way gave out the gospel message. Around 30 went out for ministry – to make first time commitments to Jesus, to recommit, for healing, for a new touch from the Lord and to pledge greater commitment to their God-given leading in the days ahead.

Sometimes things don't go according to my plans, but that's alright as long as they go according to God's plans. It's often difficult to know at the time. It was certainly the case on this occasion in the Glendower Hotel. Before the meeting began and people were coming into the hotel out of the cold, I was helping to welcome them. I noticed some unusual-looking folks, but in the excitement of the moment just before I started the meeting, I thought nothing of it. What had happened was that in my zeal to get all the churches involved, I had emailed an 'inclusive LGBT church! Some wanted to testify. This was a first for me, but these are open meetings and I do trust the Holy Spirit to guide us. Let me make it clear that I believe the Bible speaks of God's disapproval of such things. Maybe I did wrong in allowing them, I'm not sure, but at the end of the first part of the meeting I told them that Jesus loved them and I loved them and left it at that.

At the end of February we descended upon Longton Elim Church where we held a do-it-yourself meeting. I was amazed at the variety of people and testimonies which emerged in the meeting. Carl and Mandy Scott with Sheila Ede on keyboard led worship beautifully. They also testified. Others who spoke about the Lord Jesus and what He had done in their lives were Malcolm Grey-Smart (he also opened in prayer), Anna Wilcocks (FoodBank Co-ordinator), Deborah Jandles (Women Arise), Veronica Burgess (testimony of her exploits in S. Africa) and Melanie Price (absolutely mind-blowing testimonies from the UK to Romania and Hungary of people being led to Jesus). We had been praying for one of our regular folks, Papri Das Adhikary and her son, Nowel. The Home Office had been threatening to deport her and her son, leaving her husband, Panuel, in the UK. We had prayed, visited their home, sent letters of reference and attended the court hearings and now the prayers had been answered! Hallelujah! Jean decided to present Papri with a bouquet.

Two other visitors were Rev'd Sue Preston and Des Elliot from Meir Broadway Methodist Church. Their group had been praying the previous evening for some sort of Saturday evening outreach initiative in their church. Jean and I had been praying for a venue for our 30th May event the same evening after being 'let down' three times by other venues. I phoned Des later and the result was a positive welcome for UNITE to go to exalt Jesus at Broadway Methodist on May 30th!

The Elim churches had been good to us and our March event was held in their Silverdale Church. So many new folks came, too many to mention. I was so pleased that we could maintain numbers even when many of our 'regulars' couldn't make it. Our speaker was Percy Johnson who testified about coming out of darkness into light; the story of his Christian life. We touched on this at the end of Chapter 2. His experience with the witch doctor involved an empty glass filling up with blood – a sign, said the witch doctor, that Percy should sacrifice either his first son or his wife to obtain what he wanted – money!! Following Percy's ministry around seven people were prayed for.

It was now April and springtime in 2015 and a new venue had opened up for us. A few months previously, Simon Edwards had held his first 'We are Men' day conference in this church. I was there and met two lovely men of God, the Pastors of what was then 'Faithways Chapel' (now 'Gracefields'), Albert Addai and Freddie Bampoe. They were eager for us to put on UNITE in their church which had a majority of Ghanaian members. In view of this, I decided to 'stick my neck out' again and invite another man from London (remember Daniel Chand!). The man was Eric Reverence, a man born in Ghana who had also lived in Canada before moving to England. I love mixing and matching our guests and venues to see what comes out of the 'melting pot'. Eric was in the relatively early days of his music ministry and had never been to the 'wilds' of provincial Stoke-on-Trent! He wrote music and sang with his group of around seven singers. I remember one of the songs from his CD at the time called 'I Will Carry On'. I first met Eric some months earlier at one of the United Christian Broadcasters 'Leaders Meetings' in their Burslem studio. I was fascinated to see his lapel badge with the name Reverence on it! I struck up a conversation with Eric and we got on so well. We shared with each other what we did and the details of our ministries and I think it was then we agreed to keep in touch with a view to his coming to this event in April.

I am not the best at administration and logistics, but all the advertiing, promotion, arranging speakers and hiring halls/ churches is down to me. I love creating relationships by connecting Christians and getting them to meet. I love keeping in touch too. These things, together with encouraging people, are my gifts. *We have different gifts. If a man's gift is encouraging, let him encourage.* (Romans 12:8) Unfortunately, the practicalities of transporting Eric and his band from London to Stoke by train, then getting them to Hanley to their B&B, then getting them and their equipment to the church and later back to the B&B, then getting them to my friend Marcus's RCCG Church the next day and then back to London; all this became a problem I simply hadn't anticipated. The singing group were not all working and the rail fare was a problem for them. So we covered that. Then bussing them from place to place was something I hadn't thought of. I asked my friend Pastor Marcus at RCCG in Stoke if he could help, but his minibus had failed its MOT and wasn't available. However, Marcus actually hired a minibus for the weekend and provided a driver from his church to cover all the journeys! Then there was the accommodation for them all. Our good friend and supporter, Edie Hindmoor helped us put them all up in her lovely B&B, Verdon Guest House. Then they were hungry when they arrived, Pastor Albert rallied round and one of his folks cooked up a tasty dinner for them.

It all came right on the night! The powerful sound of the worship coming from the front inspired the crowd of over 90 who had come along to share in this 'City Centre' event. We locals prefer to use the town's correct name, Hanley, but in this case I'm prepared to make an exception because it describes the significant location of 'Faithways Chapel' – in the centre of the main Potteries town. Eric has a very moving testimony, but he didn't bring all of it to our event. I was looking for something to supplement the praise and worship and I wasn't disappointed. The Holy Spirit directed a friend, Lorie Whitehurst, to introduce me to two of her friends from her own Filipino background. These two ladies were missionaries to North Korea. Yes, you read it correctly, North Korea. This is a dangerous, shut-off nation, and critically so for Christians where believers can be routinely tortured to death for possessing a Bible. I cannot bring myself to describe this to you, it is too terrible to mention. In fact, I'm not even allowed to mention these ladies' names in order to afford them protection in their work. Perhaps the most poignant part of the evening was when they gave their testimonies and a video presentation about the horrendous things that happen to Christians in that nation. It was not just informative, the ladies issued a challenge to all present: "If this is what Christians in North Korea are prepared to put up with to be faithful to Jesus, what about you? Are you prepared to speak about him in your free country?"

It was a very lively evening and many gave their Christian testimonies. There were several other offers of help notably from our 'Pillar', Lydia Palmer and our friend Kevin Thompson. Kevin, a man of few words, had realised we had been struggling for transport and took me to one side after the meeting and said, "Mate, If ever you need a minibus and a driver, I'm your man!" I was overwhelmed by the goodness of so many people, and the way Kevin said this to me, almost brought me to tears. Jess Brown, an old Christian man who was a friend and mentor of mine used to use this expression which came to mind on this occasion: *The love of Christ shed abroad in the hearts of men and women.* We had such a lot of tremendous feedback for this meeting. We were honoured by the supervision of the Holy Spirit. Thank you, Lord.

At the beginning of Chapter 4 you may recall my mentioning a young Police Chief Inspector and the surprising content of his testimony. This was John Owen of Staffordshire Police. Many local people will remember him as being in charge of the major search at the Stoke-on-Trent beauty spot, Westport Lake, for the missing 13 year old Ryan Evans. Ryan was last seen in the lake "in distress" while swimming in June 2018. Ryan was found two days after his disappearance, drowned in the lake. This was a search in which much of the local community were involved, and Jon got to be known and respected by many during this tragic time. One of his comments to the press was, *"I think I speak for all services involved in the tragic death of Ryan at Westport Lake when I say it was emotionally very difficult. People often forget that those working in a professional capacity become emotionally impacted by incidents like this."* Jon is a man who is passionate about community and his job. Hundreds of mourners attended the 13-year-old's funeral at Holy Trinity Church in Burslem in July. I remember this church was formerly known as St Werburgh's and it is the church where I was christened in 1948!

I would add that John Owen is a committed Christian from the 'Evangelical' tradition. I first knew him when he was a teenager living with his parents, our friends Roger and Jeanette, who offered to accommodate me in their home when I was at a low point in my life. So I was really pleased that Jon accepted my invitation to speak at our May event. This is the event I mentioned earlier when Jean and I had prayed for a venue. Simultaneously, Rev'd Sue Preston and Des Elliott had also prayed for someone to put on a Saturday evening outreach at their church. The result was a positive welcome for UNITE to go to exalt Jesus at Broadway Methodist Church in Meir on May 30th, 2015! The Holy Spirit always puts the right people together at the right time in the right place! Have I said that somewhere before?!

Broadway Church is a beautifully designed multifunctional building which serves the community in the southern part of Stoke-on-Trent. It was built in 2008 at a cost of £1 million. So Jean was really thrilled with all the facilities, and lots of food was laid on for this event which brings us to the end of this season and the end of this chapter. We were building a very good relationship with our friends at 'Living Word' Filipino Church and many of their folks came along to this meeting. I love it when they come, mainly because they lead worship with a rare combination of fervour and reverence, but also because they bring many children along who reduce the congregation's average age dramatically!

Towards 90 people came to the meeting. We were really pleased to see some of the local Methodist folks including Ministers there. There were several Anglicans, at least one Roman Catholic, Baptists, many Pentecostals and of course the Filipino Church family! John Owen gave his heartfelt and very personal testimony. While a Christian in his earlier life, John told how some of his actions didn't always bear this out. He gave witness to the grace of God in his own life and spoke of his sister's near-death experience. I had known Jon's sister quite well many years ago, just before her illness. Then he told of his son's life-limiting condition and God's goodness and provision through all this. I think that one of the most poignant moments in the course of his testimony was how he referred to Simon Edwards, also present at the meeting. Of course, only a few years earlier, Simon, a man serving a life sentence for armed robbery, had been released on licence from prison following a life-changing born-again experience. These were two men on different 'sides of the fence'! Now, this highly respected senior police officer was actually comparing himself with Simon. He related how, when they met two years before, he said to Simon, "I wish I had what you've got". He was talking about the faith, the anointing and the passionate love for the Lord Jesus he had seen in Simon. A man was prayed for during the interval and there was plenty of testimony from the floor in the 'second half'. This was a meeting to remember and the one which will end this particular season.

CHAPTER 6

JUBILEE

Consecrate the fiftieth year and proclaim liberty throughout the land to all its inhabitants. It shall be a jubilee for you.
Leviticus 25:10

The Year of Jubilee is a joyful celebration designed to be a reminder of the goodness of God. Although the meaning of Jubilee in Leviticus 25 is 'ram's horn', it is to do with the blowing of trumpets and joyful or *jubilant* shouting and singing. This was ordained by God for the Israelites to celebrate as a 'sabbatical year' after seven cycles of seven years; a year of rest. So at the beginning of the 50th year everyone celebrated the Jubilee. A Sabbatical after 50 years. I wonder what some of our ministers would think if they had to wait 50 years for their Sabbatical!

The Jubilee, then, was a celebration of God's goodness, a celebration of freedom for slaves, a celebration of rest from work and a celebration of family togetherness. UNITE had been running for less than five years by this time, so how could we have a Jubilee of our own? We could celebrate God's goodness, we could celebrate people being set free from sin and their old lives, we could celebrate a 'rest' from the idea that salvation was something to be worked for and we could celebrate unity in the family of God. However, we had a long way to go to celebrate 50 years! But read on and see how this season of Jubilee unfolds.

We held two UNITE events in July 2015, the first being on 4th July. Although most would name American Independence as the main celebration that day, we celebrated with Bishop James Kotey at UNITE in St John's Church, Burslem! James is a good friend who travels to the UK each summer to raise awareness of his orphanage and work in Accra. He is also the overseeing Bishop of over 30 churches in Ghana. We have had the privilege of hosting him at our home each year for quite a while. We had around 90 people come to this event in St John's Church. Once again we linked in the Ghanaian influence with 'Faithways Chapel' to Bishop James as some of their worship group led us. We had two ladies, Charli and Louise, performing sign language for the deaf and much testimony from the floor before Bishop James ministered powerfully. Shortly after this meeting, Bishop James came to stay with us for a week. We really enjoyed his company and his Godly influence in our home. We had recently been invited to the RCCG conference in Manchester which was called the 'Festival of Life'. Around 8,000 folks were present, mostly Nigerians and it was a great honour for Jean and me to attend with James. It was even more of an honour to be met by my adopted son, Tunde, who himself is from Nigeria. He was a marshal at the event, and his instructions were to escort us to the very front row of the arena in front of the stage where the worldwide General Overseer, Enoch Adeboye was seated.

Our second event in July was significant for a particular reason. We had put on 'seven cycles of seven' (49) Saturday evening UNITE events since September 2011 – and you've read about them all! Now we were about to launch our 'Jubilee' meeting, our 50th, and this was to be in the Tunstall Methodist Church Hall. The Hall and the Church are all part of the same complex in Queen's Avenue, which is just to the rear of the town's beautiful Victoria Park where my brother and I spent many happy hours as boys. The marriages of my brother and sister took place in this church, as did my father's funeral. I also sang in the North Staffordshire District Choir based there, so my family has quite a connection with the Methodist Church in Tunstall. It is a relatively modern building, completed in 1975 to replace the historic 'Jubilee' Chapel – coincidence?

This Jubilee Chapel had been erected at a cost of £650 and was opened in 1788. John Wesley, on visiting it and preaching there in 1790, declared that it was "the most elegant I have seen since I left Bath". Although Jean's cousin attended this chapel, my only connection was, as a 15 year old, playing the trumpet for their production of a 'Dick Whittington' pantomime in 1963! Before its building, the church met in a house in Tunstall. In around 1783 a Methodist society was established at the house of Joseph Smith, and was part of the Burslem Methodist society. By 1775 it had 30 members and in 1787 a fund for a chapel was raised by John Wesley, the site being given by Joseph Smith. So that is the origin of the Methodist Church in Tunstall.

However, there is more to it than that. After John Wesley's death in 1791 the Methodist Church distanced itself from its roots and the outdoor preaching which he had advocated. A zealous evangelistic group arose within the society which thrived on open-air meetings (Camp Meetings) where many ordinary working people committed their lives to Jesus. They got saved! Hugh Bourne, a local man, was the instigator of this. Later he was joined by the 'fiery evangelist', William Clowes, and at the same time, Sam Barber, my 3 x great grandad! Revival had broken out! This zeal alienated the 'Camp Meeting Movement', as they were called, from the Methodists, and eventually the society expelled its steward and Sunday School superintendent, James Steele, one of the leaders of this movement.

There was a haemorrhage of fervent, significant men and women from the Methodist Society. The famous 'Camp Meetings', notably the one at Mow Cop in 1807, precipitated this and in 1911 the Primitive Methodist Church was born. Revival was going on and on! In getting started, these brave and passionate Christians aligned themselves with Clowes to hold prayer meetings and Bible classes. They didn't stop meeting together, just the opposite. Let me quote from 'The Journals of William Clowes': *'They therefore came accordingly, and James Nixon, Thomas Woodnorth, William Morris and **Samuel Barber** left the Methodist society and joined us.'* Their meeting place, and the first Primitive Methodist Church was in the house of Joseph and his son, John Smith. Sam Barber was the first black preacher in the Primitive Methodist Revival. To me, this is the best pedigree a man could ever have.

So we celebrated our 50th UNITE event on 25th July, 2015 with a barbeque and around 100 folks including six pastors came along to enjoy the food and sunshine and many gave testimony to the transforming power of Jesus in their lives. Our friend Barbara Payne, who had moved to Grimsby since we last saw her at UNITE in 2012, came back to her home church to testify and minister to us. Her message pointed to the fact that we can trust Jesus 100%. Many went out for prayer at the end of the meeting. I was really pleased that Rev'd Kim Kerchal, the new Minister at the church, stayed throughout and was, I believe, affected by the nature of the meeting – Holy Spirit presence!!

Jean and I had become accustomed to going to the Hollybush Family Camp every year, and August 2015 was no exception. Hollybush Farm (Christian Centre) held such precious memories for us. We love Pastor Jim Wilkinson, who, together with his wife Cynthia, opened up the farm in 1968 according to their instructions from God and began their astonishing ministry up there in Thirsk, North Yorkshire. I heartily recommend 'Miracle Valley', the book about Hollybush and its amazing spiritual adventures. Our 'spiritual batteries' were recharged as we sat under the ministry of Jarrod Cooper, Dr John Andrews and the long-established Northern Ireland gospel singers, 'Simple Faith'. We know so many folks there and it's a place where I have met numerous speakers who have since been our guests at UNITE. By the way, three years later, Hollybush would be celebrating their own 'real' 50 year Jubilee in August 2018 – see Chapter 10!

As August gave way to September, we prepared to celebrate another really significant UNITE event. I say significant because Daniel and Tanya Chand were to be our guests, but not only that, it was UNITE's sixth birthday! This time we had hired a newly refurbished hall in The Bridge Centre at Birches Head and managed to acquire the excellent worship band from Market Drayton Methodist Church consisting of Mark Savill, Paul and Ness Savill plus Robin and Andy.

However, Tanya had asked us to help her with a ladies' mini-conference she wanted to hold the Friday evening before UNITE. She called this 'Eden's Masterpiece' and held it in 'Faithways Chapel' in the centre of Hanley. I know that this event was extremely encouraging and helpful to the many ladies who attended. Jean was there and she told me! The 'boys' had something else to do. By 'the boys' I mean Daniel and some of his team, Brian, Asher and Isaiah together with Anthony Bostock and Dan Bailey from 'WALK', plus two rather older boys, Brett Haggar and yours truly! We prayed together in 'Faithways' and then went out on the streets of Hanley at 9pm till about 10.30pm talking about Jesus to those on their way to the nightclubs. To me, this was like 'shifting up a gear'. It was on another level. These men meant business! The prayer meeting was amazing; so much enthusiasm and real spiritual communication with the Holy Spirit. Then on the streets; Daniel's desire and ability to communicate the power of the cross to save sinners was infectious not only within our group, but to men and women who were prepared to listen. One man made a commitment to give his life to Jesus and we prayed with him. This was also the first time I had met Brett, and we got on well together. We came from similar backgrounds, both having been Police Sergeants and coming to the Lord later in life. As Friday evening came to an end, Daniel and his new wife, Tanya, came and stayed at our house while the rest of his team were put up at Verdon House, Edie Hindmoor's B&B.

We spent some time with Daniel on the Saturday as we prepared for the evening. Around 140 folks turned up for the meeting. The Market Drayton band was incredibly talented as they led praise and worship; such expertise and attitude directed towards our Saviour Jesus. Many folks gave testimony of the saving and healing power of Jesus in their lives. Daniel Chand was, once again, totally committed to preaching the free grace of God to all through Jesus Christ and His death and resurrection. He preached it with power and authority! He gave his testimony and his life-goal of sharing the love of Jesus with people present. Around forty came out for prayer at the end of the meeting. Some made first-time commitments, others recommitted their lives to Jesus. Yet others claimed healing from back pain and other ailments. 'Just one touch from the King changes everything' was the song Mark and the group sang as King Jesus graciously 'touched' His people. The following morning we went out to Calvary Church, Macclesfield, when Tanya and Daniel spoke and ministered to the congregation. Most of the church came out for prayer and many were touched, healed and changed! What a weekend!

The Autumn leaves were beginning to fall and we found ourselves back with Pastor Trevor Weaver at Bucknall Pentecostal Church for our October UNITE event. Trevor has his own inimitable style of leading worship. He plays the guitar and sings and everyone one joins in the enthusiasm and joy of praising Jesus. Our friend, Jason Abbey, who had been so helpful to Jean and me in every possible practical way was eager to give his testimony for the first time outside his own church. Trevor gave Jason a 'boost' by leading us in his favourite song, 'My Lighthouse' by Rend Collective:

My lighthouse, my lighthouse.
Shining in the darkness. I will follow You.
My lighthouse, my lighthouse.
I will trust the promise,
You will carry me safe to shore (oh-oh-oh-oh-oh).
Safe to shore.

This is a real singalong chorus, joyfully proclaiming Jesus as the peace in our troubled sea! Jason did well! A few pastors and ministers had come along and Trevor testified to a miraculous healing in his eyes. Following this, testimony flowed and Andy Tharme told how he had been over to Calais distributing Bibles to Calais for the refugees and praised God with enthusiasm as he spoke about his motivation. Following much more testimony we had our 'food and fellowship' interval before our guest, Andy Cannon spoke. I'm not going to give details of Andy's testimony at this point except to quote him as saying *"I was a drug addicted, self-harming alcoholic with three weeks left to live. I went into a rehab and someone said 'Someone here needs to give their life to Jesus'. I didn't know it was a Christian rehab, never having been to church before, but I jumped up and shouted 'That's me. I'll do it.' I went out to the man who prayed for me and I found myself shaking and speaking in another language. I didn't know what had happened until much later when I looked it up in the Bible! I'd been born-again and baptised in the Holy Spirit."* Andy's story is an amazing one, and he has since been to several UNITE events to share it and if there's space in this book I'll fill in the details later. Many were prayed for on this occasion and a good number claimed to have been healed or had a touch from the Lord.

We held two more events before Christmas in 2015, one in November at St John's and another in December at the New Life Centre in Cheadle. Throughout these two months I began to realise that if we were going to get more people to the two events planned in January, I would have to put a lot of work in circulating pastors, individual churches, the press and local radio. The two January events were now becoming an established part of our year; Biddulph Town Hall then The Glendower Hotel in St Anne's.

But back to November 2015. This was so, so special – a real cause for celebration! We actually got Pastor Jim Wilkinson at 85 years of age to come down from Hollybush in North Yorkshire to Stoke-on-Trent to speak. I was so thrilled. I just wasn't aware how well-known Jim was, as people from Manchester, Yorkshire and all over filled the church. There were lots of individual testimony and ministry before Jim spoke. In particular, a lady who had been abused as a child and as an adult and had no self-esteem came to me during the interval. She was distraught. I think this may have been triggered by my own testimony about my daughter being intimidated – I felt so much for this lady, but passed her to Pastor Lydia to minister to her and to link up with her in the following week.

The theme which rang out through the evening was "There is power in the name of Jesus". Jim Wilkinson spent time speaking of this power in testifying of God's goodness over the last 70 years in his life and ministry. The story is in the book, 'Miracle Valley 3'. There was more ministry at the end of the evening by Jim, myself, Lydia and others and we ended the meeting at 10.30pm. I spoke to Jim on the phone a day or so later and he said *"Keep doing what you're doing, bringing the Christians together and encouraging them to keep talking about Jesus. Nobody else is doing what you're doing!"*

It was 5th December when we held our Christmas UNITE event in Cheadle (Staffordshire). There was a Christmas tree, great worship music from Scott Calvert and the band, 'O Holy Night' sung beautifully by Jill Eckersley and, of course, the amazing Terry Eckersley! Terry certainly didn't disappoint as he gave a Christmas story with a new twist: Good News; Great Joy; Seeking Jesus! Old but ever new! There were a number of young men present and Terry was just the right man to pray for and encourage them in their Christian walk. We experienced some wonderful prophetic insight by Bryan Johnston who said that revival is much talked about, but in reality it was starting at UNITE in Cheadle. This had been confirmed earlier in the day by John Stanway. John has now gone to be with the Lord. There was confirmation of Bryan's prophecy by way of a message in tongues from Gail James who spoke of how the purity and beauty of godliness was being obscured by our worldly ways and perceptions, but in seeking Jesus we find good news and great joy!

Once again, Christmas came and went but not without much work in circulating our upcoming January events. It was 9th January, 2016 and the Town Hall in Biddulph was packed just like last year! As I mentioned previously, Biddulph is the town where our own church is situated and because a prophet is without honour in his own town, I always underestimate the number of people who will be interested in attending our first event of the year! I needn't have worried. So much went on in this meeting, it's almost impossible to include it all.

This was to be an evening consisting of very much down-to-earth testimony – to say the least! No niceties; except for the completely contrasting Christian dance put on by the very young Filipino children who had come with their parents from 'Living Word' Church. Several of these parents were leading worship for us once again. A young man with a vulnerable nature who was bullied at school testified, and his 'teacher', Miss Barlow was in the audience. This was our lovely Christian friend, Debbie Barlow. She had stood up for him and encouraged him at school. His testimony made her cry. She was not the only one! Adam Longshaw gave a great account of how sharing his faith at work caused him to be in danger of losing his job with the NHS. At a later tribunal Adam was accompanied by Ismael Mendoza, a work colleague who is also a Christian and was with us at UNITE this evening with 'Living Word'. His daughter was leading worship. Ismael later confirmed that Adam was reinstated, and at the tribunal Adam told the other delegates that they needed to receive Jesus!

Beat Mueller gave a very moving testimony. His wife, Marlene, went to be with the Lord three weeks earlier and it was her funeral the day before this UNITE event. Beat testified to the timing of the process of her passing that she was able to see her son from America when the medical opinion was that by that time she should have died. Much prayer followed during the interval. These intervals are precious times for fellowship and one-to-one prayers.

I mentioned previously that at these meetings, where all are invited to participate, we can sometimes find things happening which we really would not have planned! So, in case anyone thinks all our meetings go smoothly and according to plan, they don't! It's just as well really, because we depend on the leading of the Holy Spirit to bring the right folks in to share the right testimonies at the right time. A young man I'd met who had been in rehab with Simon's WALK ministry was brought to the meeting. He was drunk. One of the WALK men asked me whether they should bring him into the hall or not. I said "What would Jesus do?" He came in but we made him promise not to speak. Of course he did speak. I was at the front running the meeting and the man shouted out from the back of the hall. After a little amusing but sincere banter, the WALK 'bouncers' got him to sit down quietly. He was an alcoholic. Now this is how the Holy Spirit works. There was another man in the hall who was in his sixties. He stood up and told how he became an alcoholic when he was younger. This was our very good friend and prayer warrior, Bryan Johnson. He then prophesied over the young man saying that he would overcome his addiction. I am aware that the young man did overcome the addiction and he certainly had a fervour for the Lord Jesus. I have lost touch with him now, but I do look forward to hearing his testimony sometime at a future event.

Christine Lewis testified and ministered in the second half. She gave a moving account of her troubled relationship with her father and of how she ran away from home aged sixteen and fell pregnant. Her ministry acknowledged and reflected the raw nature of the evening's events and testimonies. Christine also highlighted the conflicting characteristics of the new Spirit of God in the believer and the soul which brings in the old wounds and self-justification to fight against Jesus' will for our lives. She described how she was delivered from an inherited generational spirit of anger. Definitely led by the Holy Spirit, she ministered along these lines. Many went out for prayer at the end of the meeting!

The City of Stoke-on-Trent has a coat of arms which contains the motto *'Vis Unita Fortior'* which translates as 'United Strength is Stronger'. This is a message which UNITE has been trying to put out to the churches and Christians since its inception. Actually, the real message is that unity is good and pleasant in the sight of God. He brings strength and blessing when His people accept His gift of unity and put it into practice. Stoke-on-Trent people have long been known for their warmth and kindness, but mention Stoke City and Port Vale and watch the antagonism surface! The 'Potters' and the 'Valiants' supporters are anything but united! Maybe that was at the back of my mind when I booked the 'Carlsberg Suite' at the Crewe Alexander Football Club for our UNITE event on 20th February 2016. Crewe is only 13 miles 'over the border' into Cheshire and for this occasion, Jean and I became 'Alex' supporters! I even sang 'Blue Moon' which is the anthem sung by Crewe Alexandra's fans at the matches. Of course I put my own Jesus words to the tune! Jesus' Church transcends all barriers!

A really good crowd of around 150 from all over Cheshire joined with folks from Market Drayton, Bolton and Stoke-on-Trent to give Jesus glory for the amazing things He had done in people's lives. This superb venue was just right for all that went on during the three hours of testimony, praise and ministry. The testimonies were brilliant; so spontaneous and heartfelt. Here's an extract from a Facebook comment:

Well what a great night last night at Crewe Alex football club. Some brill life stories of people's lives being completely turned around and healed. One lady shared about her son who was heavily into drugs and she didn't expect him to live for long because of his heavy use and life style. But guess what... he came to know Jesus and he was completely set free from all of that life threatening stuff. He's now telling others about Jesus in prison (coz he had to do some jail time just after) and how they also can be set free! One guy was into self-harming. Not just cutting himself with knives, which is bad enough, no. This guy threw acid on himself. He came to know Jesus and his life was transformed. Peace flooded his life. Another Dad shared about his new born baby. The doctors said he wouldn't live. There was no way unfortunately. This was on Good Friday 3 years ago. After a number of requests from the Dad the doctors finally agreed, Dad could go and pray for his son. His son came out of hospital on Easter Monday with a clean bill of health! Others who were in trouble with the law ended up even advising judges etc. One was heavily into illegal fighting just so he could get some money for his Mum. All these came to know Jesus.

The worship group from Rugeley Victory Church, headed up by Matt Tyrrell, was inspiring and created a very receptive atmosphere. Peter Gladwin was our speaker, once again and he was 'on-fire'. Following his appeal at the end, one young man gave his life to Jesus following a word of knowledge from Peter. I prayed with him and look forward to seeing a turnaround in his personal circumstances. Then Peter prayed for those who stood up to receive spiritual empowerment; most of those present! I scored this event a home win for Jesus!

I have often held 'Men's Breakfasts' in venues around the City and on 12th March 2016 I put one of these on in St John's Church in Burslem. These events have always proved to be valuable for men to share problems, be prayed for and encouraged in their Christian lives. On this occasion Andy Cannon drove down from Liverpool for our 9.30am start. Andy is always half an hour early for any event he speaks at. After a superb breakfast (thank you, Lydia and girls!)

Andy encouraged us all to invite our Christian friends to get a team together to go out on the streets of Hanley the following month to share the Good News of Jesus Christ with the shoppers and anyone who would listen. He called this 'Empowered Evangelism'. This Good News is best summed up by an old song I once heard at Hollybush Christian Centre. It goes:

Joy, joy, joy in my heart is ringing
Joy, joy, joy Jesus keeps me singing
Singing of His mighty love for me
Telling how He died to set me free
Filling all my life with melody
Joy, joy, joy!

Jesus had put a new song in our hearts; we were going to tell people about it! In the meantime we held a UNITE event in Silverdale on 19th March. Will Graham, Pastor at Victory Church, Rugeley, came to speak. Will said that he had travelled the world with the good news that Jesus saves souls and heals bodies. However, he then shared that only last month, after a lifetime of good health, he had suffered nervous exhaustion. After feeling physically and emotionally drained, Will believed God was saying to him *"I value you more than I value what you do."* After prayer and rest, Will regained his health and he was certainly on top form as he ministered, encouraged and prophesied over people at UNITE. His message was that God puts greater value on us than we often think. Will interspersed his talk with prophetic messages for at least six folks in the meeting. The prophecy I remember best is the one he gave to Aimee Scoffins. Aimee, who loved the Lord Jesus, was a very shy young lady who lived with her parents. I was so pleased that my daughter, Caroline, came along that evening and made friends with her. It seemed almost incredible when Will prophesied over Aimee saying words to the effect that she would travel by plane and boat and train to distant lands to take the Gospel message of Jesus Christ. Surely Aimee was last person we would expect to do that. Don't let us despise prophecy, please read on and see what the Lord can do with anyone who makes themselves available! We will discover what the Lord really did in Aimee's life in Chapter 10. It's not your *ability*, it's your *availability* which God is interested in!

There were around 100 present, and our friend, Lorraine, brought a group of people who came to the Crewe event last month. This included two ladies who had only been saved two days. Another young woman saw UNITE's website, contacted me and came along for the first time. Her feedback came by email:

Dear Cedric and Jean,

I just wanted to send an email to let you know again how much I enjoyed last night, it was the first time I have attended a service like this and it uplifted my spirit completely, thank you for making me feel so welcome, I will look forward to seeing you both very soon.

Testimony flowed from many in the gathering and there always seems to be a Holy Spirit leading in a particular theme. The theme of much of this was that God had given confidence to those without any and propelled them to achieve the things which they had previously thought impossible. I appealed for folks to join in Andy Cannon's 'Empowered Evangelism' initiative and nine came forward joining six from the previous week's Men's Breakfast. Pastor Edwin, once again, was so gracious and encouraging in allowing us to use his building and facilities.

Let's take a break before we move into April 2016, our visit to 'Miracle Valley' the much anticipated visit of Andy Cannon to join with us in 'Empowered Evangelism' in Hanley and the testimony of a Circuit Judge at UNITE in Swan Bank Church, Burslem – plus other celebrations to follow!

SELAH

CHAPTER 7

OTHER CELEBRATIONS

They celebrate your abundant goodness and joyfully
sing of your righteousness.
Psalm 145:7

The week before we joined Andy and the team in Hanley we were invited to 'God's own Country' (Yorkshire – remember, God is a Yorkshireman; that's because He's always right!) I guess Jean and I were on a new level of faith and expectancy as we travelled up to North Yorkshire to Hollybush Christian Centre on 14th April, 2016. Pastor Jim Wilkinson had invited UNITE to take the main part of their Friday evening meeting. This was a great honour for us and the furthest we had travelled outside of North Staffordshire to hold a UNITE event. We took Joan Adams with us and Cliff, Lottie, Veronica Quaile and Ann Grainger travelled separately. That's seven 'Pillars' to support the platform the Lord was giving us; remember the one from heaven where Jesus was to take centre-stage!

We had a tremendous time praising and worshipping the Lord in the unique Hollybush style! I managed to get some folks out to testify or just even share a few troubles. This is how the Holy Spirit works in these meetings. A lady came to the front to share her great concern for her grandson who had just got into some serious trouble with the Police. This led to Veronica testifying to God's intervention in her son's criminal life from his almost certain death in St John's graveyard to his decision to give his life to Jesus and his totally transformed life. Don't give up hope! This was an encouraging Holy Spirit message to the lady, without doubt.

Ann Grainger was our speaker and her message from 2 Chronicles 20 was excellent; King Jehoshaphat's victory: 'Do not be afraid or discouraged, the battle belongs to the Lord'. The message really gelled with a number of the earlier testimonies. It was, as always, a glorious evening in the presence of the Lord at Hollybush. I never cease to be amazed at how God's people are able to encourage and minister to one another even when they have never met before. This is how God blesses when His people come together in unity.

It was only a week later when Saturday morning, 23rd April, 2016 arrived and 24 folks gathered in 'Faithways Chapel' in the centre of Hanley for the previously mentioned 'Empowered Evangelism'. This included Andy and a few of his friends from Liverpool including Chris Moran and many UNITE supporters. I was thrilled that my daughter, Caroline joined us for this. After an encouraging word from Andy we all went out into the town to be part of Jesus' 'Great Commission'. After a few minutes, one of the first people I spoke to was a man from the 'Unite' Union who was giving out leaflets. After he gave me his message, I gave him my message: *"God loves you and Jesus died for you to set you free to spend eternity in heaven with Him. Will you turn from your old life and live for Him?"* Quite to my surprise, he said *"Yes."* We then prayed together. Another coincidence? The Unite Trades Union. We later gathered again in 'Faithways' and reported back, rather like the 70 disciples who returned to Jesus and said *"Even the demons are subject to us in your name."* I don't remember any demons being cast out in Hanley that day although I don't rule it out. Many had been led to the Lord Jesus by the Gospel message and in prayer and we heard several reports of healings. This was a great encouragement for us and it propelled us to hold outreaches in all the Potteries towns in future months and years. We ended with a tumultuous 'Hallelujah'! We were to repeat a similar but much larger Gospel adventure in the future with Andy and his team in the spring of 2018. Read all about it in Chapter 10.

Yet another week later, on the last day of April we were back in the 'Mother Town' of Burslem holding our 60th UNITE event in Swan Bank Methodist Church. That was a cause for celebration! The minister, Ashley Cooper, had always been very good to us and had generously allowed us the use of the main church on this occasion. We had a remarkable turnout of around 150 folks and this included my daughter, Caroline. Swan Bank is a big church building and looked pretty full on this occasion. Some months earlier I had got to know a man called Graeme Smith, a Circuit Judge. Graeme is a member of Alsager Community Church and a fine man of God. I thought how different it would be to have someone who wasn't an ex-drug addict, ex-criminal or ex-prisoner testify at UNITE about Jesus! Graeme gave a lively and relevant testimony in the 'first half' to which many could relate and it set the scene for the 'second-half' testimonies. These revolved around Graeme's theme – with man it's impossible, but with God all things are possible. Testimonies of abuse, depression, lives restored to Jesus were flowing.

We saw many new faces and there were some great testimonies on this occasion. A young couple who had been recently divorced came to the meeting to testify that they had become reconciled to each other and were to remarry. This was specifically the answer to much prayer by some of the 'Pillars' over a period of time. One young woman told everyone present that by prayer to Jesus she had overcome depression and suicidal tendencies. But that wasn't all. She met her sister-in-law for the first time in two years on this night. There had been a family rift and they hadn't spoken during that time, but reconciliation came during the interval at UNITE!! This was spontaneous and exciting! That's what we're here for; uniting, reconciling, restoring – under the headship of Jesus.

An amazing thing happened at the end of the evening and I only discovered this the following day. Sarah Abbey was prayed for by Cliff and Lottie Roberts. Cliff, a long-distance lorry driver, had suffered a condition called trigeminal neuralgia; it is serious, very painful and chronic! This was before Cliff was saved and became a Christian. His sister said why don't you ask Jesus to heal you? Cliff scoffed, but he was desperate and he did ask Jesus, saying that if He would heal him, he would serve Jesus all his life. While still a week away from home he threw away his tablets and discovered that his incurable illness was cured! Praise Jesus!! Cliff has faithfully followed his Saviour and healer ever since. So Cliff prayed for Sarah and Sarah was healed also. Thank you Jesus! From taking 32 tablets a day and still being in pain, Sarah now had no pain and no need for tablets. A little later in the year and in this chapter, there was another reason for Sarah to celebrate. Please read on.

At the end of May, 2016, UNITE was back in Tunstall Methodist Church Hall. This was a smaller meeting with around 65 attending. We were greatly encouraged by 'Fresh Breeze Choir' from 'Faithways Chapel' who led us in worship. They had also done this so well last month in Swan Bank. Our friend, Adam Longshaw was the speaker for the evening and he related how his employers at the NHS decided to discipline him for offering to pray for a patient at his place of work. He was able to trust God to bring him through and even prosper him in all this; and this is exactly what God did. This was the 'full' version of the testimony Adam gave in Biddulph

Town Hall at the beginning of the year. Corporately we prayed for Adam and his wife, Mel. I should mention the surprise visit by the 'Glory Man', Nigel North from Leicester, who gave us some lively renditions of the old gospel songs accompanied by his accordion!!

On 2nd July (the day after my birthday!) we held UNITE in Longton Elim Church where we met the new pastor and his wife, now our good friends, Paul and Lynne Dunne. They had just moved from Yorkshire (God's own country?) and I think this was one of their first evenings in the church. A good crowd of folks had come, some from as far away as Birmingham. An old friend of mine also lives just down the road from the church. His name is George Salmon and he and I used to hit each other in our younger days. Let me explain. George was a professional boxer, but before turning professional, he and I boxed together as amateurs. I had a few minutes to spare before the church opened so I phoned George and invited him along. To my delight and surprise, George appeared in the church. I got him to the front and he told the crowd how he had accepted Jesus into his life and become born-again. However, before this he pointed to me and said to the people, "See this man, I beat the hell out of him!" – in a good-natured way, I hasten to add. Bishop James ministered powerfully as always and at the end of the meeting there were many people lying about on the floor following prayer. I thought, what if this new Pastor isn't too keen on this sort of thing! I need not have worried, Paul and his wife were appreciative of this move of the Holy Spirit.

Our next celebration was to be, yet again, in our Burslem base, St John's. As it was 25th July and high summer, we held our barbeque in the grounds; thanks again to Cliff and Lottie. Around 100 folks came along to enjoy the sun, food and fellowship as people spread about in the spacious grounds. Incidentally, only a few yards away stands Pleasant Street, rebuilt in the 1960s, but originally the home of my great, great grandparents, Isaac and Martha Barber and Isaac's mum, Frances – the widow of the famous black preacher I mentioned earlier, Sam Barber. All these ancestors of mine worked in 'The Pots' and Burslem was the world centre for ceramics in their time.

Our guest speaker was our friend Christopher Dryden. A highly intelligent man, Christopher gave his testimony speaking eloquently and very sincerely about his life and how Jesus had brought him through many challenges. His theme was 'What does God do with broken pieces?' Without going into great detail about this particular UNITE event, in the middle of the meeting, a young woman who was afflicted by a demon, or unclean spirit, was brought to the front. A few of us prayed over her and expelled that spirit in the name of Jesus. A young Polish man who couldn't speak English told us how God had sent him to Europe to take the gospel message to Polish people. How did we know this when he spoke in Polish? We had an interpreter on hand! So there were a few unusual things going on; nothing unusual about that at UNITE!

Looking through Jean's 2016 diary I saw that we had some very hot days during the summer, if I interpret the word 'Scorchio' correctly! For some time I had been asked by the BBC to travel to London on 28th July to take part in an interview with David Olusoga for his television programme 'Black and British: A Forgotten History'. This was to take place in Dr Johnson's house in Gough Square, off Fleet Street, and was because of my direct 4xgreat grandad, Francis Barber who was 'adopted' by Dr Johnson. I wasn't too keen on travelling there that day as Jean and I were due to drive up to Yorkshire soon afterwards. Not only that, but I feared I might get lost in the big Metropolis, a place I would willingly use the Tube to get about when I was young. However the BBC were very persuasive and provided transport to and around London. I was so glad I went. David Olusoga and the team were excellent. David is a very warm and sincere man and we spent a number of hours recording for the programme. I was also made very welcome by Celine Luppo McDaid, the Curator of Dr Johnson's House, who told me I would be unveiling a plaque in memory of Francis Barber outside the house a little later. So that's what happened. Oh, I forgot the champagne reception and all the dignitaries. I was actually made to feel quite important. Ironic really, that the descendant of a slave should be given much more honour than the slave himself! Obviously this was a significant event and a number of black students were also present. After my short speech, a young black lady came up to me and said, "Are you a Christian?" I said "Yes", she replied "So am I", I said "Hello sister!" I didn't get any champagne, but I was driven by chauffeur back to Victoria Station where I took the train back to Stoke.

I got home late that night after being stranded outside Stoke Station for a while. But I was so pleased I'd gone. That was Thursday 28th July. I'm referring to Jean's diary again and I see we took to the streets of Kidsgrove on Saturday 30th to share the gospel message. I think one man made a commitment to Jesus on that occasion. On Sunday 30th July Jean and I travelled north to Harrogate where we stayed in a B&B while attending the European Leader's Advance Conference in the Harrogate Convention Centre. This was an exciting time for us for many reasons, not least to be able to see Heidi Baker, Bill Johnson, Randy Clark and Paul Manwaring However, one of the first people we met was Andy Cannon who was 'in respite' after an exhausting evangelistic tour in Europe! It was precious to experience the amazing ministry of Heidi Baker, but no less so to unexpectedly bump into other friends at the conference, namely Iris Barcroft, Jonathan Conrathe, Pastors Paul and Lynne Dunne, Alison and Martin Macklin and Will and Kathryn Spendilow.

Following an excellent few days of teaching, praise, fellowship and worship at the conference we travelled 25 miles deeper into 'God's Country' arriving at Hollybush on Wednesday 3rd August – a few days into their annual Family Camp. The 'trademark' Hollybush worship was in full flow as we arrived; it really draws us into the spirit of praising Jesus! John Andrews was teaching each morning and Jarrod Cooper was speaking in the evening so we were being well-fed! In addition we again met so many Christian friends – including Bishop James Kotey! However, allow me to digress a little. When we're back home, Jean tells me that I always talk to other people on the bus. That's partly true. But if I meet an African or Jamaican, I definitely speak to them. I love to identify with those who come from the same nations as my own forebears. I talk to them about Jesus and my experience is that they are much more receptive than most white people. Why am I telling you this? One evening in 2015 as I travelled home on the number 7 from Hanley, the bus was crowded. A young lady was sitting next to me and I struck up a conversation with her. She was originally from Kenya. I told her that I was a Christian and that I was trusting in Jesus for my salvation, how He died, rose again and is coming back for those who believe. Why am I telling you this? This same lady was present at Hollybush in August when we arrived. A God-incidence? Maybe, but we were privileged to see her baptised in the River Wiske which runs through the field belonging to Hollybush Farm – 140 miles from home!

We enjoyed our summer of 2016, but at the end of September we were preparing for a special celebration, the fifth birthday of UNITE.

Yes, it was five years since our first Saturday evening event when we wondered if anyone would turn up. On this fifth birthday event we hired the 'Valliant Suite' at Port Vale Football Ground. We became Vale fans! By this time, Evangelist Daniel Chand was gaining quite a following of young Christians who were hungry to see God move in their generation. Daniel and I had an unwritten agreement that he would come to speak at UNITE each September. So Daniel was our guest speaker for the evening. He liked a band which was based in Liverpool, so we arranged for them to come down to Port Vale. It was not the Beatles! Actually this worship band consisted of many of Andy Cannon's close relatives. They were inspiring. We also brought Tracey Simpson of the Billy Graham Evangelistic Association (BGEA) to give a presentation, so there was lots to fit into the evening. The 'Valiant Suite' began to fill up and I was thrilled to see my beautiful daughter, Caroline, walk through the doors. She had come along with our friends from Market Drayton, Malc and Steph Grey-Smart. We had over 150 people there from Birmingham, Bedford and Liverpool. Jean had put on an amazing spread of food for the interval.

One of the challenges which we often encounter is the balance between the time given to praise and worship and the invitation of testimonies from the floor. I don't have too much control over this, and I am glad about that. The Holy Spirit was in control on this evening as He had been so many times before. Praise and worship continued well into the 'first half' leaving not so much time for testimonies. However, I believe the balance was just right.

A man called Charles Baden was first up relating how he had studied and studied and studied the Bible trying to get doctrines spot-on and be perfectly correct in every way. He had met Daniel Chand some time previously and had seen that signs, wonders, healing and salvation were taking place whenever he ministered. Charles wanted to pick fault with this and criticise Daniel, rather like some had done when Daniel was with us two years before. However, he decided that he would discover what it was that Daniel had got that he hadn't. It was the personal empowering of the Holy Spirit, the very presence of God manifested by loving others as God loves them!! This testimony was so right to start the evening. Aimee Scoffins was brilliant testifying about the great things she has seen recently on mission in South Wales. Remember the prophecy Aimee had received at UNITE in March? However, this was only the beginning for Aimee! Two years later she had a very exciting account of her evangelistic work in Mexico, but that's for chapter 10!

So, appropriately, after the interval came the 'second half' at the Valiant Suite, Port Vale. Daniel Chand was inspired as he testified and spoke out the radical Gospel truths which lead to God moving powerfully among His people by His Holy Spirit. The simple Gospel message proclaimed by someone who is 100% trusting God is powerful.

'Then the disciples went out and preached everywhere, and the Lord worked with them and confirmed his word by the signs that accompanied it.' Mark 16:20.

From our point of view, we also believed that as God's people had gathered together in unity (from all the denominations and churches) this was the place where the Lord would command a blessing this evening.

'How truly wonderful and delightful to see brothers and sisters living together in sweet unity! . . . For from this realm of sweet harmony God will release his eternal blessing, the promise of life forever!' Psalm 133: 1-3

Yes, there were people who came to Jesus for life everlasting at the end of the evening, but before that something absolutely amazing happened. I have always believed the passage prophesied in Isaiah 61 which Jesus revealed one Sabbath in the Nazareth Synagogue as being fulfilled in Him.

"The Spirit of the Lord is upon me, for he has anointed me to bring Good News to the poor. He has sent me to proclaim that captives will be released, that the blind will see, that the oppressed will be set free, and that the time of the Lord's favour has come." Luke 4: 18-19.

I had seen the poor receive and respond to the Good News of the Gospel, I had seen prisoners transformed and their lives turned round and I had witnessed people held captive in sin and addictions set free – all by the power of God. However, I had never witnessed the blind receive their sight. Jesus had added in verse 21:

"Today this scripture is fulfilled in your hearing."

Two good friends of ours were there, Jason and Sarah Abbey. They had helped us tremendously with the practical side of things. As Daniel was proclaiming the truth of the scriptures, I discovered this was being fulfilled in my hearing too! We actually witnessed Sarah being given the sight back in her right eye. The camera and microphone were on Sarah who had been blind in this eye since she was two years old. She shouted out and cried as she saw her husband, Jason, for the first time through this eye!! A miracle of healing. I'd never witnessed anything quite like this before. There were many shouts of 'Hallelujah' ringing out in the room. Rather than try to describe the atmosphere, let me give you this YouTube link: *https://www.youtube.com/watch?v=iJoAYjefxLg* It's all on there! Another lady received feeling back in her hands after years of numbness and a man claimed to be healed of depression there and then. We felt so blessed to celebrate our 5th Birthday in Holy Spirit style!

As we approached autumn, we held another three UNITE events before Christmas, 2016. On 15th October we were pleased to be hosted by our beloved Filipino friends in their church at Normacot (Longton). The small Mission Hall was filled to capacity, the food was out of this world and testimony after testimony thrilled the folks present as they heard what Jesus had been doing in people's lives. Notably, Jay Lee from Tunstall spoke powerfully about his recent conversion to being a born-again Christian. His confidence and assurance were a great encouragement to us all. Pastors Carl and Mandy Scott had a 'slot' where they led worship and shared testimony. Mandy's testimony affected many folks there. The question of the homeless came up chiefly because of seeing a number of them during our Saturday morning Gospel outings. Sheila Walton and others had met and spoken to a number of men without homes. They shared their heartfelt concern for these men and we continue to make connections and help in any way we can.

Earlier in the year we met a man called John Lawson from East Sussex, an intelligent and very interesting man with a rather chequered background. John had held a book signing session in W H Smith in Hanley for his 'true crime' book, 'If a Wicked Man'. This is how one reviewer described the book:

'It tells his gripping life story. John Lawson had a reputation among the gangs and violent men running the clubs where drugs and prostitution were rife. A mercenary of brutality and crime, he repeatedly found himself in prison. . . where he eventually met God and began to transform his life.'

I wanted John to come to UNITE. I read his book and wanted him to come even more. I also wanted to link up with another Newcastle-under-Lyme church as we had only ever held events in that borough at Silverdale Elim. Jean and I went along to the Sunday morning services at Newcastle Baptist Church where we were warmly received. The facilities there were excellent and there was enthusiasm for our proposal to bring John there for a UNITE event. So it was arranged for 12th November.

It was great to see the church filled with around 100 folks. Worship was led by Matt Tyrrell (a talented singer/songwriter now living in New Zealand) plus Danni and husband, Majek. There was no shortage of testimony, and it was fresh, vibrant testimony of God making a difference in schools, Christians out on the streets helping the poor and homeless, giving out the Gospel and making a difference in ordinary folks' lives. I was aware that John's testimony and ministry was going to be very forthright and direct; no nonsense. I had seen him deliver the gospel to great effect on a previous occasion. John is a British born Christian Evangelist but in his former life he was a violent criminal who gave his life to Christ in prison in 2005. He was also a leader and trainer within the Great Commission Society (GCS). Their vision statement is *"To communicate the Good News of the Gospel Message relevantly to every person in all the world."* By 'coincidence' Eric Reverence is the Executive Director of Media & Communications of this organisation. Tony Anthony, author of 'Taming the Tiger' is the CEO. I have made contact with Tony with a view to his coming to UNITE at a later date. John's presentation was methodical, believable and receivable, and at least one person in the meeting received Jesus as his Lord and Saviour.

And so we reach the last UNITE event of 2016, the end of this season of 'Celebration' and the end of this chapter. Our last meeting of the year was on 3rd December. This gave me the opportunity for advertising, planning and preparing for our two important January events in 2017 before the 'Christmas rush' got underway and no-one would be interested in the New Year! Last December we had Terry Eckersley speak for us at the New Life Centre in Cheadle, this December we were privileged to have our young friend, Tim Lucas, as our guest. Tim was the Church Liaison Officer for Stoke-on-Trent's 'Saltbox' charity, which connects churches and does much valuable work across North Staffordshire. Tim shared some of his testimony in the context of Mary and her 'story' in the circumstances surrounding Jesus' birth. He included the folks present, suggesting that we all have a 'story' of circumstances which, while we may not fully understand them at the time, God does.

The 'second half' saw Vicky Gardner giving her testimony. She has been through so much in her life but has come through so strongly this last year or so. She loves Jesus and she greatly encouraged us all. Bill Foxall, who never usually gets up to testify, told of his amazing healing from cancer and gave credit and glory to Jesus. Some more really encouraging prophetic messages came from the folks from 'New Life' and also from Malcolm Grey-Smart who had travelled all the way from Market Drayton to celebrate with us!

CHAPTER 8

PASTURES NEW

Yes, I am the gate. Those who come in through me will be saved. They will come and go freely and will find good pastures.
John 10:9

2017 was a 'New Pasture' for us although we began the year with two UNITE events in familiar surroundings! However, we did have a few new venues in mind and also a few quite famous names to come and speak. Mixing 'business' with pleasure, we ventured out into Lincolnshire for a UNITE event in June while we were on holiday. We connected with a few new churches and, more importantly, the people in them! We were making new connections in the 'body of Christ', His Church. Remember; 'Connecting and Encouraging Christians; introducing people to Jesus.' It occurred to me that our intention was to embrace God's gift of unity among 'blood-washed, Spirit-filled Christians'; those whose hope was in Jesus Christ alone for the forgiveness of their sins, their Salvation and their eternal home in God's presence. What if people came along who were Christians in name only, could we be united with them? What about those who did not know Jesus as their Saviour and Lord? Firstly we put out the message very clearly; our hope is in Christ alone, his death, resurrection and ascension. We fully believe that He then sent the Holy Spirit to gift and empower His present-day disciples. So we aimed to bring people fully into this Salvation, and by testimony and the Gospel to lead those seeking into a relationship with Jesus. That was it, in a nutshell.

Now let us allow the Lord to make us lie down in the familiar green pastures of Biddulph and Lytham St Anne's for our January events before we move on to the still waters of Kidsgrove and Longton!

The hard work was over, the circulations and advertising had been carried out and many were invited by word of mouth as 7th January approached. Would we get a full house in the Biddulph Town Hall? Earlier in the day, Luke and Nicola Vardy arrived at our home and we enjoyed getting to know each other. We had spoken over the phone and I knew this was a married couple who were 'on fire' for Jesus; just what we were looking for! So in the morning they joined with us and some of the UNITE team taking the Gospel onto the streets of Biddulph and telling folks about the evening event. Two of our ladies prayed for an arthritic lady and led her to Jesus! The new Methodist Minister, Nick Witham, came and encouraged us and allowed us to use his church building to meet before going out. This was a good informal way for our new Pastors, Mark and Liz Holdcroft, to get to know Nick.

The evening arrived and there was a definite buzz in the Town Hall as our, by now, annual UNITE meeting took place. As was our practice, we took a group into the kitchen to pray before the start time of 7pm. When we returned to the main hall it was packed with around 170 folks. I was so pleased to count around six pastors or vicars in the gathering, one of these being Rev'd Steve Dyson, the new vicar of St Lawrence's Church in the town. This was a show of interest from among the denominations. We were led in worship by 'Living Word' Filipino Christian Fellowship. Some of the very young girls from 'Living Word' performed a dance to some beautiful Christian music. Dave and Jacky Kidwell gave a presentation of their ministry to the homeless. They called this 'Essentials'. They brought along a lady called Tam. She had been living on the streets and they had been able to find housing for her. They also testified of a homeless man in Hanley who had 'died' in a doorway, but they were able to give first-aid and pray for him. The man is now alive!! Many other encouraging testimonies followed.

In the 'second half' Luke Vardy shared testimony and ministry in a more powerful way than we have seen for some time at UNITE. We were so thrilled to be able to hold up this platform for Jesus to minister through such a young, enthusiastic, spirit-filled, on-fire man as Luke! At least four committed their lives to Jesus at the end of the evening. One was the former homeless lady mentioned – Tam! Another was Phil, a man who came in deaf in both ears but received his hearing from Jesus when Luke prayed for him. Many folks came from far away, including Sarah Dale who spent the day with us after joining us on the streets in the morning. Sarah lives in Chester and we are honoured to see her whenever she manages to attend our meetings.

A few days later we were heading north once again for the Glendower Hotel in Lytham St Anne's. As with the Biddulph event, all the advertising had gone out; local radio, newspaper and all the local churches. We arrived on the Thursday to enjoy Christian fellowship and the bracing sea air (I use the word advisedly, it was blowing a gale!). We took our friends, Joan, Sheila and Margaret with us to join around twenty other Stokies at the hotel. Some of these are from the Salem Methodist Church in Smallthorne and others from Trentham Parish Church. They are ladies who have become very good friends over the years. They love the Lord Jesus and I know they have a brilliant time in St Anne's. I should also mention that the sales in Blackpool are quite an attraction for them!

On the Saturday, 14th January we had around 60 come to the event, a little down on the year before, but as Jean says, "God will send along who He wants to be there"! I was satisfied with that. Our good friend, Steve Moss, pastor of Fylde Christian Service Church in St Anne's started the evening with a bang! His enthusiasm was electric as he and the band led worship. Some great testimonies followed from Christians from such different backgrounds. One man called Philip testified to being 'born-again' in Singapore in 1948. Another testimony came from Trish, a former alcoholic and self-harmer who received Jesus only recently. Peter Cunningham from Bolton was there testifying too. It's always good to see Peter. Judith Mackay from Blackpool sang 'God on the Mountain' beautifully for us. Judith has become our regular guest singer and we are thrilled and privileged to have such a warm and sincere Christian with us. You may remember that Simon Edwards' name first became known to me while we were holding a UNITE event in St Anne's in 2013. You will probably remember too that he spoke at the Glendower the previous year (2016). This year (2017) Simon and his wife, Karen were among the audience, having stayed in the hotel for a well-earned break.

Our speaker for the evening was our friend, Christine Lewis. She mixed some testimony with a message based on 1 Peter 1- turning to God, being sprinkled with Christ's blood and turning away from the 'empty way of life inherited from our forefathers'. Many were prayed for and ministered to at the end of the evening. The following morning we added around 20 folks to Steve Moss's church where, as always, we had a great time.

On 25th February, 2017, we were led to a new pasture! It was the old Methodist Church in Kidsgrove. The church had been decommissioned by the Methodists and the complex of buildings sold to a Muslim man who had converted part of the premises to a solicitor's office. However, the main building, which had been the church, was intact although very run down. Our friends, Pastors Carl and Mandy Scott, had rented the building, renovated, improved and decorated it after hiring it from the owner. Over twenty years before, I had preached in that church (known as Kidsgrove Cathedral!) when I was part of the Methodist Connection. But that's not all, fifty three years before, I used to go there to a youth club, so it held many memories for me. This UNITE event also happened to be our 70th!

The place was buzzing, people were dancing and worship was beautifully led by Matt Tyrrell. This is a big building and it looked full. There was an abundance of testimony. Remember Jacky Kidwell from the January UNITE event in Biddulph Town Hall? She reminded us of the young lady they found homeless in Hanley before Christmas. Following this, the same young lady, Tam, gave her testimony of being saved by Jesus in the Town Hall. Terry Eckersley spoke commandingly on 'Don't deny the Power' which happened to be the title of his latest book! He was referring to the power of the Holy Spirit in the name of Jesus. Two people committed their lives to Jesus on this night. The following morning in the same church, Terry spoke again and we were thrilled that a man who had been going to the church for a short time made a true commitment to Jesus.

Our next UNITE event was to be on 15th March in Longton Central Hall and to some it may appear that we were heading into the political domain. However, nothing could be further from the truth. The man we had invited was formerly Minister of State for Defence Procurement and Chief Secretary to the Treasury in John Major's Cabinet. Unfortunately he was convicted of perjury and imprisoned.

Why would we want him to speak at UNITE? I will explain, but not yet! First I want to tell you about a journey I made into new pastures, and not exactly voluntarily! Remember the Trentham Ladies who support us at St Anne's? They are very persuasive, and while we were with them in January, they 'ganged up on me' and talked me into being a model at their annual fundraiser, a charity fashion show. I couldn't refuse, could I? It reminded me of an amusing little announcement made in a church announcing something similar: *Ladies, don't forget the rummage sale. It's a chance to get rid of those things not worth keeping around the house. Don't forget your husbands.*

So on 4th March I found myself dressing up in 'pre-loved' attire in the Meir Heath and Rough Close Village Hall. It was quite a well-attended event. Lots of ladies were there to see me strutting my stuff on the catwalk to the delightful commentary of Radio Stoke's Lamont Howie. Of course, it gave me the opportunity to show off my Norman Wisdom pretend trip! It also raised a few laughs and a considerable amount for worthy charities.

March 15th arrived and my adopted son, Tunde was commissioned to collect our guest speaker from Stoke Station. In the meantime I was struggling to obtain sound equipment, projector and help to provide the best for the evening. It was at this time, not long before the meeting was due to start that my friend, Peter Turner, said to me "The Lord is with you". This was a profound blessing to me because I knew it came from a sincere and godly man. In the event, Glenn Parkes, Jeff Short and a 90 year old man from the church got us sorted out and Paul Critchley together with his talented daughters led worship. We were 'on a roll' as the evening began and I introduced our guest. I haven't told you who this aristocratic yet disgraced politician was who received a life-changing encounter with the living Lord Jesus while in prison. It was, of course, Jonathan Aitken. At the time of writing (2020), he is an ordained Anglican priest, and the Chaplain of Pentonville Prison.

Jonathan was very well received. Witty, amusing and theologically sound, he gave testimony of how he received salvation and encouraged those present to 'come on this way' of following Jesus. John Brough (Jean's cousin) was there and I think he was more affected by Jonathan than any other speaker he had heard at other events. This was followed by an excellent Q&A session. Some great testimonies followed. One was from a convicted murderer who had served a life sentence. Another was from Pastor Mike Cummins who'd travelled up from London for the event. Mike has been a faithful prayer warrior for us especially through his programme on Revelation TV. The Lord Mayor of Market Drayton came (thanks to our friend and supporter Malc Grey-Smart) as did Godfrey Davies, the recent prospective Parliamentary candidate for Stoke South. Much prayer was given at the end of the evening for some needy people!

Spring had arrived once again and in April 2017 we held two UNITE events. On 7th, we put on UNITE in the Friday evening Hollybush meeting. While this is not 'new pasture' any more, it is a working farm and surrounded by fields, livestock and rural life. We arranged to stay at Newsham Grange Farm which is a favourite B&B of ours and less than a mile from Hollybush. In addition we had our friends Barbara and John Payne stay at the B&B and Barbara was to be our speaker for the evening. Sally, Lynn and the worship group were 'on form' and so was Jim! I have such admiration for him as a man and as a man of God. We began with an introduction to UNITE and then invited testimonies. Unexpectedly, during this, a video was projected. I had no idea what it was, but it turned out to be that of

Sarah Abbey receiving her sight last September at Port Vale UNITE! There was no shortage of excellent testimonies; glory to Jesus! Then Barbara spoke. This was mostly testimony but with some really good biblical backup. She ministered at the end and many, many went out for prayer and received from the Lord. Christine, a lady who'd come with Barbara, and was in constant pain from arthritis and taking 8 to 10 'Co-codamol' tablets per day, was healed on the night. No more pain, no more tablets. God is good! We were privileged to take UNITE to Hollybush once again and we have been invited back!

On 29th April we were thrilled to be invited to hold UNITE in Rhema Mission Church, Rode Heath, just over the border into Cheshire. This church was established by our friend, Pastor Ray Holdcroft and is now led by his son-in-law, Pastor Simon King. So while we knew them well, it was a new venue for UNITE and therefore new pasture! We feel very warm towards the fellowship there and were so pleased that around 100 folks came along to the event. We joined in some really lively worship, Simon's wife, Alison, leading (many of the band were absent with sore throats!) There was some good testimony from friends of UNITE, Gerald Gleaves, Phil Vyse and Donna Yates which added to the family feeling of the evening. Our guest speaker was Pastor Matthew Murray from 'Renew Church' in Uttoxeter. Matthew gave an amazing account of a miracle healing in his own life from malaria. He also told the heart-rending story of how he and his wife, Becky, began their ministry, 'One-by-One' in Kenya. Very briefly, it goes like this: In Kenya, Becky sees a little girl without shoes. Becky buys her some shoes. The little girl follows Becky round asking if she needs her to accompany her to her hotel. Becky eventually realises that the girl only understands that gifts are normally given in exchange for sexual favours!! How sad. When I first read this testimony I was left in tears. At the end of the evening, in a beautiful ministry session, many were prayed for and given words of knowledge.

Another outcome of our January UNITE event (apart from my catwalk experience!) was the suggestion from the 'Trentham ladies' that we should hold an event in their church, the Parish Church, St Mary and All Saints. This was a 'good pasture' for us to get to know more of the Good Shepherd's flock in the historic area of Trentham which was described in the Domesday Book as a Royal Manor with one priest! I thought that, since all true Christians are a 'Kingdom of Priests', it would be appropriate for UNITE to 'graze' in that pasture where we would lift up the name of Jesus and pray for people! As we always do, Jean and I visited the church and joined in their Sunday service to have fellowship and get a feel for the venue. So on 20th May we set up in the church for the evening UNITE event. Rev'd Andy Morgan was really helpful and led lively worship with the church band. Our friends, Iris Barcroft and David Finn (each Church Wardens) helped us with the practical arrangements. When 7pm arrived the church was filled to capacity with Christian folks from all over the Midlands publicly sharing the goodness of God in their lives.

This is what I recorded following the meeting: *There was much testimony from the floor during the 'first half' including Cliff Roberts who shared about his work with 'Reach', meeting the needs of the homeless. Cliff had a message for Christians which was 'If you are burdened with a desire to help others you should get up and do it!' Our guest speaker was James Adams from Stoke-on-Trent, winner last week of the Outstanding Public Engagement Category of the prestigious Making a Difference Award for Social Responsibility, 2017. At 23, James has overcome a severe health scare to set up services for teenagers with cancer. He is currently heading a huge project in Burslem to help homeless, hopeless and vulnerable local people. Having shared his own Christian testimony, his message to Christians was that if they feel strongly that something needs to be done, then get up and do it! This was an echo of Cliff's earlier exhortation! James encouraged the church to get behind such projects to help those less privileged than themselves. Once again, the Holy Spirit brings harmony to the messages given when we meet in unity!*

Just to summarise, the project James had begun in Burslem is now fully funded and set up and it's called 'Number 11'. If you hadn't already realised, James is the third 'headcase'! (Chapter 4) He spoke so well with real motivation and gratitude to God for all the prayers which brought about his healing from the brain tumour which, five years earlier, had threatened to halt his school work and subsequent career. He is now a fully qualified doctor. This was a most encouraging evening in the presence of God.

Two weeks later, Jean and I travelled to more distant new pastures. We travelled 186 miles up to South Shields. It was the birthday of Andrew James (another one of the three 'Headcases!) the following day, Sunday, 4th June and we planned a surprise visit to him at 'Living Waters Church' where he was due to take over as pastor. We stayed in a slightly mediocre B&B in South Shields, waking up to television reports of the aftermath of the shocking terrorist attack on London Bridge where eight people were killed. Despite this, we were able to enjoy a peaceful walk along the beautiful beach at South Shields. We surprised Andrew and his wife, Gail, at the church, enjoying a time of worship there before they invited us to their home for a tasty barbeque Sunday lunch. Driving north for another 55 miles we arrived at an exquisite B&B where we were to stay a few days before moving on to ever more new pastures! The B&B, St Cuthbert's House, is a tastefully converted former Presbyterian Chapel in the small village of North Sunderland – 60 miles north of the better known City of Sunderland. North Sunderland is a fishing village on the coast of Northumberland and adjacent to Seahouses. We enjoyed this beautiful time together so much, walking the mile or so to Seahouses with its old-fashioned quaintness and excellent fish and chips! It was a great pleasure to meet our good friends from our home church, Eric and Tina, who were staying in Newbiggin not too far away. Jean had arranged this with Tina, and Eric, a real Geordie, who originally came from the area, as evidenced by the way he aspiratedly pronounced Seehoooses!

During the week we drove to Bamburgh Castle, took a boat trip to the Farne Islands to see the puffins and spent a day in Alnwick. New pastures indeed! While we were in Alnwick, I received a phone call from Barbara Payne – remember, she spoke at our last Hollybush UNITE meeting. We had arranged to stay with Barbara and her husband, John, later that week in Grimsby, 200 miles away! While speaking to Barbara, I asked her where she was. She told me she was in Alnwick!! A 'God-incidence'! So we met up and the four of us spent some quality time together in that beautiful market town – almost in Scotland. We arrived in Grimsby as scheduled on the Thursday and stayed with Barbara and John for almost a week. They were excellent hosts, feeding us well and taking us on some amazing days out. It was a privilege to be with them. One remarkable memory was going to see Brother Yun at the Civic Hall in Cottingham, just outside Hull. Brother Yun's book, 'The Heavenly Man', tells both of great persecution, and a surprising series of miracles of deliverance. Despite a life of poverty in China, he since has spoken to thousands internationally with the Gospel message. Seen as a rebel among some Chinese for not joining the government-controlled Christian organization, he was imprisoned and tortured by the government authorities. This event was organised by Jarrod Cooper's 'Revive Church' and the first person we saw when we arrived in Cottingham was James Seager, one of the admin team there. Actually, James is originally from Biddulph and a former member of our home church; we know him and his family well. Another 'God-incidence'!

I'm leading up to describing a meeting which was held in Barbara and John's house. Actually there were a number of meetings there through the week where Christians and non-Christians came together, got to know each other, shared testimony and talked about Jesus. Barbara had suggested we held a UNITE meeting in the house on the Saturday. So we did. What an amazing opportunity to invite testimony from so many relatively new Christians. Twelve of us gathered together in Barbara's home and shared stories of how Jesus has changed our lives. We explained what UNITE does in Stoke-on-Trent and there was an immediate enthusiasm to get involved. We met a married couple, Tony and Angie, managers at a homeless project called 'Knotted Note' in Grimsby. They were not Christians, but during the meeting became very interested in the teachings of the Lord Jesus and we felt that they would soon make that commitment. On this occasion, Barbara's much valued and highly effective ministry was born; 'Women Unite', our 'sister ministry' which has been held on several occasions in Grimsby and Stoke-on-Trent. We had no worship band, but John started up a few old hymns, and we all joined in! We also arranged for Barbara to come down to speak at UNITE on 9th December at St James' Community Hub in Newchapel, Stoke-on-Trent.

Summer 2017 was now underway and we had three UNITE events lined up in three new venues – or new pastures! The first was in the prestigious Herbert Minton Building in Stoke. The second was our own church, formerly Biddulph Pentecostal Church, now renamed 'Life Stream Church'. The third was the main auditorium at the Bridge Centre in Birches Head.

I had been a trustee for the RCCG Living Water Parish for many years and Pastor Marcus had this year successfully negotiated the purchase of the Herbert Minton Grade II Listed Building in Stoke. This is an historic and culturally significant place for our good friends at RCCG to take over for their church and Christian work in the city. Here is an extract from a newspaper report which I sent to the Sentinel Newspaper:

Herbert Minton would have been thrilled to see the crowd gathered in the former Grade II listed Arts College in Stoke on Saturday. Many Christians came along to UNITE's latest event in this magnificent venue to acknowledge Jesus, sing lively praise songs and listen to the guest speaker, Christopher Dryden. Christopher spoke on 'being a misfit accepted by God.' Minton China exported to countries all around the world and later diversified into tiles. The amazing floor in the White House, USA, is one of Minton's prestigious achievements. That so many nations were represented at the UNITE event in the Herbert Minton Building reminds us of Stoke-on-Trent's rich and skilful ceramic heritage. Herbert Minton financed the building of Holy Trinity Church, Hartshill, in 1842, and his nephew, Samuel Minton, was the first vicar of St Thomas Church in Penkhull. So it was fitting that a church, the Nigerian Redeemed Christian Church of God (RCCG), eventually bought the premises this year. The UNITE team thank Pastor Norah Chilaka for hosting their event.

There were many new faces present and much of my effort went into bringing together two particular churches, one in Hanley ('Faithways') and the other in Stoke ('Living Water'). By now you may have realised that these two churches were made up of Christians from Ghana and Christians from Nigeria. Even though there is only a mile-and-a-half separating them I was unsuccessful in drawing many from Ghana! I even took a football and suggested a match between the two countries to spark some interest, but as it turned out, I might as well have tried to unite Stoke City and Port Vale supporters! However, around 130 folks came along. There was much ministry and corporate prayer from Christopher at the end of the meeting.

It was 22nd July I was another year older! This was the day for our annual barbeque event and we were to hold it for the very first time in our home church. So we were very familiar with the church – Jean and I had attended since 1997, and in 2000 we were married there. But for UNITE, this was a new pasture! Hitherto, I had not felt motivated to hold an event in our home church for various reasons, but on this occasion we were excited! Our new pastors, Mark and Liz Holdcroft, joined us and some of the UNITE team in the morning, in Biddulph, taking the gospel of salvation through Jesus Christ to the folks in the town and letting them know about our evening UNITE barbeque event. Our guest speakers, Martin and Claire Thompson, also arrived to help us tell people about Jesus.

Martin, Claire and their children, Lewis and Sophie, piled into our house for a really good time of fellowship. Before we knew it, it was time for the BBQ to begin and, once again Cliff and Lottie did us proud. Apart from a few drops, we avoided the rain which had been forecast. Come 7pm, extra chairs had to be put out for the 150 or so folks who turned up for the main event. I was particularly pleased that we had managed to get such a large number into our church at this time. I knew Mark and Liz would be encouraged. The evening began with praise and worship from Liz and the band followed by testimonies from the floor. These flowed abundantly until it was time for the interval.

In the 'second half' Martin and Claire testified and ministered and many were touched by the Holy Spirit. Some were healed and at least one – a teenage girl – committed their life to Jesus. Groups of Christians came from Crewe, Leek and Congleton and I was thrilled to see Pastors Mandy and Carl Scott and Paul from Kidsgrove Grace and Faith Church, particularly so as they prayed and prophesied over Mark & Liz. I felt this was good 'bonding' between the two churches. The place was 'buzzing' once more. Even so there was quite a number from the home church who didn't come along. However, we were excited. Because of Martin's ministry, a good number from around the city returned to hear him the following evening.

It was by now late July and the Hollybush Family Camp had begun. However, because of a friend's 65th birthday celebration and a 'Daughters of the King' event at Mandy and Carl Scott's 'Grace and Faith Victory Church', we didn't head north until Monday 31st July – four days into the camp. The atmosphere, as always, was electric; Jesus was being lifted high! Fellowship was amazing, we met several friends, Paul and Helen Wellington and Mike Nibbs from Crewe, Bishop James Kotey from Ghana, Neal and Noreen Hall from Western Australia and Barbara and John Payne from Grimsby plus many, many more. Speakers at the camp were Dr John Andrews, Peter Cavanna, David Jones and Jarrod Cooper. We really find this Family Camp so inspiring and encouraging in the middle of a busy year. Everyone is so upbeat and thrilled to talk about

Jesus. Here's a little quip to illustrate:

Someone once said there are only two kinds of people in the world. There are those who wake up in the morning and say, "Good morning, Lord!!", and there are those who wake up in the morning and say, "Good Lord, it's morning!"

Our great time of fellowship in the presence of God soon passed and so did our short tour of the Yorkshire dales. Before we knew it we were heading back to Stoke-on-Trent. However, we would be returning to Hollybush six months later to put on UNITE at one of their Friday evening celebrations.

In a similar way to our last event in Biddulph, we held our 30th September UNITE meeting in a familiar venue, the Bridge Centre. We had hired the premises the previous year to host Evangelist Daniel Chand. We were doing the same again now in 2017, however, this time we had been given the privilege of using the very large main auditorium. I say 'privilege' because we asked to hire the very well-appointed smaller room because of its lower cost. In the event, the smaller room was not readily available and we were given the larger room for the same price! God had blessed us. So we were in a semi-new pasture!

We estimated about 200 folks came along from as far away as Newcastle-on-Tyne to London and all over the Midlands. We had problems with the sound as Pete Clarke and the band from Liverpool struggled with earphones and feedback. Our friend Arthur Reeves did his best with the projector even though lacking the words to some of the songs. In addition we experienced a domestic situation which arose just before the start and police visited during interval! However, we realised that this event was important to the enemy (Satan) and he would do what he could to distract people. His plan didn't work! We got underway with a testimony from Sarah Abbey – her sight was restored to her right eye when Daniel prayed for her last year at Port Vale – Sarah was brave to testify about her recent separation from Jason and their ongoing reconciliation. She loves Jesus!! John Douglas was there; remember him from Biddulph Town Hall, Jan 2016? He's been struggling with heroin and alcohol again but he came along sober and in his right mind. He didn't volunteer to testify, but Bryan Johnstone who had previously prophesied over him came out and testified to the miraculous healing from cancer of Pastor Mike Cummins following prayer. Pastor Mike lives in London and is one of our UNITE Prayer Warriors. After Bryan had testified, I asked John to come out and he shouted "Glory to Jesus!"

Daniel testified and ministered in the 'second half' and his theme was that we should keep persisting in our faith for more than we can ask, think or imagine, making reference to the Syro-Phoenician woman (Mark 7:25). In a general prayer he prayed for healing and one young man claimed his back pain was gone! He then prayed individually for around 50 who came out for prayer. Daniel's brother, Sharman, spoke a word of prophecy directed to someone named 'Rose'. Remarkably I was standing next to Rose Smith who was with her friend, Rosalie Bromley, both from St Jame's Church in Newchapel. Daniel then prayed for her and she fell on her back. I caught her head as I was aware she cannot lie flat. After some minutes I helped her up and she said with great surprise and joy "I wasn't expecting that!" Many reports of Holy Spirit activity came to me in the days and weeks following.

Time for a break in the middle of a busy season! After our 'Selah', we'll be exploring more new pastures with more new speakers – including the man who made 'Doo wah diddy diddy dum diddy do' famous! They don't write them like that anymore!

SELAH

CHAPTER 9

OTHER PASTURES

We are His people, the sheep of His pasture
Psalm 100:3

The leaves on the trees in our garden began to turn golden brown as autumn approached, and on Saturday 28th October we put the clocks back one hour. I had always been confused as to whether they went forwards or backwards, on one occasion turning up two hours early at 4am for a morning shift! But the maxim, *Spring forward, Fall back* has always helped me since! On this same evening in 2017 we held UNITE in 'The Lighthouse' in Burslem.

We arrived at the rear of the Lighthouse after a disastrous Port Vale home defeat to Swindon thinking all the crowds had gone. Wrong! A far right rally in town had attracted protesters and several arrests were made. Nevertheless, around 80 folks turned up to celebrate Jesus in this old Congregational church. Scott Calvert and his band from Cheadle led worship and there was no shortage of testimonies. In addition we had a 'Heart4Truth' presentation from Michael Bellamy of Sheffield. This is an initiative to train churches to counsel people with mental and emotional problems. Andy Cannon was our guest speaker. Andy was soon due to go to Nigeria to be approved as an evangelist by Reinhard Bonnke. He gave a great word encouraging us to go to people with the gospel and be led by the Holy Spirit to those in our sphere of life. He prayed for many at the end and several were touched by God. One lady who came into the meeting very gloomy went out radiant. During the prayer at the end another lady let out a prolonged scream as Andy ministered to her. She also left the meeting radiantly!

On 18th November we celebrated our 80th UNITE event in Meir Park Community Centre in the south of Stoke-on-Trent. I noted at the time, "I never thought we'd get to 80 UNITE meetings!" This was a new venue and a new pasture for UNITE.

The venue was the meeting place of Pastors Rob and Em Price's 'LoveStoke' Church. A difficult place to find in the dark! Several reported in the following days that they returned home not being able to find the centre! However, around 80 came along. The Filipino Christian Fellowship from 'Living Word' were with us so numbers were up from the outset! Their usual worship band led us initially, followed by the younger musicians (youngest 12 yrs) – they were brilliant! Alec Gapuz gave an impassioned plea to trust in God through the difficult times. A number of testimonies from the floor followed including those of Brian Porter and Steve from Liberty Farm. How God has transformed the most problematic lives! Beat Mueller also testified and Cliff Roberts spoke about 'REACH' Ministry at the Salvation Army in Stoke. Luke Vardy and his wife Nicola followed in the 'second half' beginning with Nicola's testimony in brief. This was truly powerful. Luke followed through with a great message on the Holy Spirit empowering us to give out the gospel message, to pray for the sick and see God really working in our lives – we need to ask, seek and knock. Several were prayed for towards the end and Jason Abbey had prayer for his broken foot which he hadn't been able to move. Jason took of his foot support and was able to move his foot for the first time since his accident.

St James Church at Newchapel was the venue for our 'pre-Christmas' UNITE event. Jean and I grew up in Newchapel and we now live a stone's throw from this significant 'Church on the Hill.' I am inspired to see its steeple pointing towards the heavens every morning from my prayer room. We had held an event in the church a few years earlier, but this time we achieved our ambition of holding our meeting in the new Community Hub built adjacent to the church; a new pasture! This had been a long time in being completed, but it was a lovely building.

In the bleak mid-winter, only around 40 people made it through the snowy conditions on 9th December! These included Malc & Steph who had driven all the way from Market Drayton! The slippery, snow-covered car park was valiantly manned by Dave Phillips who later joined us in the meeting. Rev'd Janet Arnold, the new vicar at St James, also came along. It was great to introduce Janet to Pastors Charles Machin and Jim Lowe and also to Malc and Steph as they are from St Mary's Anglican Church in Mkt Drayton. Our speaker was Barbara Payne. Barbara had travelled down from Grimsby and was staying with us for a few days. She felt a spiritual connection with Janet and told me she felt that we would be working with her in the future! The worship group we put together was Nancy Phillips, Kerry (from St James worship group) and Alex McClean – they were excellent with choruses from the 90s that everyone knew.

Barbara spoke on 'spending time at the feet of Jesus.' She was effective in communicating this message to the 'all-Christian' audience especially for the times we are living in. Many came out for prayer and ministry by Barbara. Alex was suffering a very painful and debilitating back condition which he testified later had been vastly improved giving him mobility which he had not had before. Much testimony followed from people like Cliff Roberts, his wife Lottie , Malcolm Grey-Smart and not least Rev'd Janet Arnold who gave the background to her taking up the post at St James, "do you fit the bill for the church on the hill?" In fact, Janet was the first to get up to testify and I was very impressed by her participation. The meeting was a smaller but significant and intimate gathering of Christians and was really effective in bonding people and denominations.

This was the 'run up' to Christmas and although we had held our last UNITE event of the year, there were several other meetings which we led locally on behalf of our own fellowship, 'Life Stream Church' in Biddulph. It's easy to forget about these regular meetings, many of which were held in older folks' residential and nursing homes. We had held these for several years and it was only by glancing through Jean's diary which brought them to my mind. In fact, over several years we had seen towards 50 older people make commitments to invite Jesus into their lives. This was a very satisfying contribution which Jean and I had had the privilege to make. In looking through Jean's diary I also saw that we were out in Tunstall the following week taking the gospel message to those in the streets. These outings were a regular feature of our Christian work in the Potteries towns and again, we saw many make first-time commitments to accept Jesus. Jean and I also ran a weekly meeting at our church called 'Tuesday Venue'. Our special Christmas meeting including Christmas dinner was arranged for the following Tuesday (12th) and we had arranged for Christine Lewis to speak. Unfortunately she couldn't make the meeting because of the snow. Neither could Barbara get back to Grimsby because of the snow, so she took Christine's place, extending her stay with Jean and me a further few days. Her ministry was brilliant; God's answer to our problem! However, once more before the 'Christmas rush' I was busy advertising our New Year UNITE events and encouraging folks to come along.

On the coldest night of the year we presented our first UNITE event of 2018. This was in our, by now, regular venue of the Biddulph Town Hall. Around 100 came to this meeting, noticeably fewer than last year, but a really good evening all the same! Possible threatened disruption from certain quarters didn't materialise! For some reason the laptop and projector we were expecting hadn't arrived. However, our friend Adam Elkington soon remedied that; we were all sorted electronically! These matters were both answers to considerable prayer! 'Answer to prayer'; This seemed to establish the theme for the evening. We began with the superb, hyper-dedicated, enthusiastic praise band from Leek Gateway Church. Adam Elkington led the band, and people were prepared, eager and expecting the immanent presence of God. Becky Murray was our guest speaker and spoke in the 'first half'. Becky and her husband Matthew, are pastors at 'Renew Church' in Uttoxeter and they head up 'One by One' Ministry. This is a missionary organisation with a heart for the poor and broken across the Third World. Back in April 2017, Matthew spoke for us at a UNITE event in Cheshire and told us why the ministry began. On this January evening Becky related the details of Matthew's miracle healing in Kenya. This is how Matthew's book, 'He still Heals' puts it, 'Given just three hours to live by the medics, Matthew Murray was on the very edge of eternity when his wife, Becky, put out a desperate call among her Facebook friends.

#PRAY4MATT went viral, and instead of dying his body began to battle against the disease. Matthew's amazing recovery from multiple organ failure is a real life testimony to build faith, even in the midst of despair.' This was, without question, answer to prayer! Becky's message was inspiring and encouraging to the attentive audience

The testimonies which followed were along the lines of God arranging circumstances in the background while preparing us for action; the action he wants from us. Our faithful friend Malcolm Grey-Smart brought my daughter, Caroline, and another lady called Christen to the meeting. He always has so much of God in his life and is always seeing people at strategic times; and seeing them give their lives to the Lord! Christen is a lady he and his wife, Steph, met on the canal and to whom he spoke about Jesus! Jonathan Howard enthusiastically testified of how God supplied his family's financial needs in a most miraculous way! This was a good start to 2018!

Once again our annual seaside UNITE event was almost upon us and only four days after our Biddulph meeting a car-full of us headed north once again to Lytham St Anne's. We arrived in the welcoming Glendower Hotel at noon on Thursday giving us opportunity to meet up and have fellowship with the various groups also travelling from Stoke-on-Trent. Sightseeing, walking, shopping in the sales and relaxing are also high on the list of our UNITE followers. I am personally allergic to shopping and I don't relax easily, but I arranged a meeting over coffee in the Glendower Hotel with our friend, local pastor and our UNITE worship leader, Steve Moss. We sat, talked and more than anyone else in recent years, he counselled and compassionately ministered to me. Thank you so much, Steve. He is a valued friend of ours and a true man of God.

I had invited Tracey Simpson, a representative of the Billy Graham Evangelistic Association (BGEA), to give a presentation on the Saturday evening. Tracey had previously spoken at one of our events in Stoke-on-Trent and she was keen to come up to St Anne's. In the course of advertising our event, I had spoken to one of the local pastors who was leading the initiative to bring Franklin Graham to the Winter Gardens in Blackpool later in 2018. He asked me to be sensitive in our advertising because of a certain amount of opposition to Franklin Graham in the Blackpool area and particularly from one of the local LBGT churches. I wonder if we had met them three years before! This opposition mushroomed to the extent that a petition was raised to ban Franklin and two local MPs were also voicing their dissent. The basis for their disapproval was that Franklin was homophobic (prejudice or dislike of homosexuals) and Islamophobic (prejudice or dislike of Islam or Muslims). The fact was that he was coming to Blackpool to preach the love of God and salvation through Jesus Christ. This BGEA event was to be a big one!

From our point of view we were putting on a UNITE event to bring Christians together from all their different backgrounds and to share the gospel with any who did not know Jesus. Around 80 turned up for the event – the numbers gradually increasing year on year. Steve Moss and the band were brilliant, Steve leading worship very beautifully!! Judith MacKay sang two lovely songs, 'One Day at a Time' and 'My Forever Friend.' I always find Judith's singing very moving. Several powerful testimonies came from the audience, many about God's plan outworking in people's lives. It was Steve's birthday the day before so we sung 'Happy Birthday' to him and bought him a little gift!

Andy Cannon was our guest speaker and he occupied the 'second half.' He gave some amazing testimony and encouraged us to be bold in sharing Jesus with people. This was very effective and many came out for prayer, mostly for boldness in witnessing. A young lady called Rachel was in tears at the end. I spoke to her for some time, sharing personal things we had in common. On her way home with Elana who had brought her, she gave her life to Jesus! This is the kind of response I love to see at UNITE events; individuals being motivated to be part of Jesus' Great Commission! Elana goes to Steve Moss's church and we saw her next morning and she told us all about Rachel. I also discussed the possibility of Steve coming to Stoke-on-Trent to speak to a Pastors' Breakfast meeting we had decided to arrange; he was agreeable. What a great weekend!

In February, 2018 we held two UNITE events, one in Yorkshire and one in Cheshire. Neither of these were in 'new pastures' as such, but they were outside our home area. I was always wary of depriving Stoke-on-Trent of a monthly UNITE meeting, but as you'll soon discover, we more than made up for this in March!

Our first February outing was on 16th at Hollybush Christian Centre in North Yorkshire and we took 'Pillar' Joan and our friend, Lorraine. What a privilege for us to take UNITE to 'Miracle Valley.' Jim Wilkinson made us so welcome! We experienced the unique 'Hollybush sound' to help us praise God and take us into His presence, followed by some great testimonies from the floor about the life-changing power of Jesus. This could not have been more evident than in the testimony of Aimee Scoffins who, together with a number of other young folks, had driven over from Revive Church in Hull. Aimee was confident and full of the Holy Spirit as she told us of the changes Jesus had made in her life. She used to be very nervous and lacking in confidence. Jesus changed all that. The prophecy she received from Will Graham at UNITE in Silverdale back in March 2016 had been fulfilled exactly. We gave Aimee the opportunity to give this testimony more fully later in 2018 on 'home territory' and we'll find it in the next chapter. Luke Vardy was our speaker for the evening. What a vigorous Holy Spirit message he gave about being sold out for Jesus! Luke's wife Nicola also gave testimony so powerfully and their children, Isiah and Atlanta (aged 10 and 12) prayed for the sick at the end of the evening. A lady with a back problem found her leg growing by half an inch!

On 24th February we were really pleased to be back in New Life Church in Congleton, Cheshire. This meant that so far in 2018 we had held UNITE meetings in four different counties! This was part of the prophecy given over mine and Jean's lives in 2004 by Pastor Jim Wilkinson when he said that we would go from town to town in England to give out the gospel message. A good number of folks (around 120) came along on a cold night, but things soon 'hotted up' as our guests, 'SIMPLE FAITH' gospel singers got started! They were amazing! Only two voices, Paul Cairns and Jonathan Welsh, but what power – natural and supernatural. They had the audience dancing!! With song, testimony and an appeal, God moved two people to give their lives to Jesus and two more to return to Him at the end of the evening. There was also some excellent testimony from the floor and this was recorded on camera by David Green of Christian Television.

While 14th March 2018 did not take us to pastures new, we were taken up a level by the celebrity status of our guest speakers/ singers! In a way, we were in new territory holding UNITE on a Wednesday. I was a little concerned about this; would folks come out in Kidsgrove on a weekday? Kidsgrove is on the edge of Stoke-on-Trent and not as accessible as most of our other venues. However, I wanted to do this locally and particularly to get people through the doors of Pastor Carl and Mandy Scott's Grace and Faith Victory Church. This was a 'SPECIAL', our guests being the famous Paul Jones (Manfred Mann and his own pop music successes) and his TV presenter, actress and singer wife, Fiona Hendley. We were amazed at the turnout – around 200. We were also taken aback at the variety of those attending. A man from my schooldays whom I had not seen for over 50 years came because he saw my name in the paper advertising the event and wondered if it was me! Others came out of curiosity and many Christians from the city arrived in addition to some from Blackpool! I heard several say "I've brought my husband along; he'd never come through the doors of a church normally!" As we began, Sarah Abbey, still in her carer's uniform, walked in. Immediately I gave her the opportunity to testify to the crowd how Jesus had given sight to her blind eye! I gave a rendition of 'Doo wah diddy diddy' but to my own words! Then Paul and Fiona came on. They were exceptional! Beautiful singing of blues/gospel songs and amazing testimony of God's grace in their lives. Paul related that, as a former atheist, he argued with Cliff Richard about God on TV, but later went with Cliff to a Louis Palau convention and received Jesus. Fiona put over the gospel message passionately and accurately. This was probably the best presentation to a crowd of this variety I have ever heard. At the end, Paul and Fiona gave out cards for folks to fill in. Many received these cards and completed them. There were three boxes to tick; one to receive Jesus for the first time, another to recommit and a third for a prayer request. This was very successful. They promised to pray over these cards for one week and then return them to me. Quite a lot of prayer was going on by the team at the end. There were around five new decisions for Jesus, many recommitments and very many requests for prayer; one of these from my daughter, Caroline who had come with our friends Malc and Steph. Together with so many others I was so thrilled with this event and had some astonishing feedback.

Before venturing with UNITE into other pastures deep in the Staffordshire Moorlands in April, we did something else new. This was to hold our first breakfast meeting for Pastors and Ministry

Leaders. The idea was to bring them together to get to know each other, keep in contact and hopefully begin to work together in God's Kingdom in Stoke-on-Trent. So on Saturday morning 14th April, around 30 ministers, pastors and vicars from several denominations met for an excellent breakfast in the specially set aside room in Hanley Baptist Church. I wanted someone from outside our area to speak, and after breakfast and individual introductions, our good friend from Lytham St Anne's, Pastor Steve Moss gave an encouraging and highly motivating message. If you remember, a few months back in January, Steve had agreed to speak for us. In the meantime, Andy Cannon pressed me to allow him 'five minutes' to introduce an evangelistic initiative he had in mind. When evangelists use figures to describe the length of their talk, it's like me estimating the number of folks at our meetings! However, Andy was true to his word, and he successfully motivated many of those present to get involved in a gospel outreach in Hanley (Stoke-on-Trent's City Centre) the following month. I was extremely pleased with our first Pastor's breakfast meeting. It would be true to say that there were some present who had ministered in churches only a few miles apart for many years who had never met each other. If you turn back to the first few sentences in the Introduction of this book you will be reminded of the relevance of the desert island story!

Easter had passed, and it was time to take UNITE to 'Gateway Church' at Leek in the Staffordshire Moorlands on 21st April, 2018. I had tried hard to involve the various local churches in Leek to join in with this event. I don't think I was too successful in this, but around 85 people from all over the North and Midlands turned up. On a warm, sunny evening with the double doors wide open, the Gateway Church resounded with some amazing music from Adam

Elkington and the band as people praised God and shared how Jesus had changed their lives. Our guest for the evening was Peter Cavanna whom we'd met many times at Hollybush Camp. Peter is a very focussed but also humorous speaker. He began his career in entertainment, heard the gospel in a theatre and then became a Christian, teaching at Mattersey Hall, one of the country's foremost Bible colleges. He spoke passionately about the importance of forgiveness in our lives referring to Jesus' parable in Matthew 18, saying that it was an 'injustice' that Jesus suffered and died to pay for our sins and the sins done to us. Peter stressed the need for us also to forgive those who had hurt us, even though it doesn't seem fair. Many were affected by this message and responded by coming out for prayer at the end of the evening.

Apart from getting Christians together and introducing people to Jesus, another of UNITE's aims is to link people in strategic ministries. A team of six students from Mattersey Bible College, a ministry from Grimsby (Barbara and John Payne) and a group from Uttoxeter 'Renew Church' came along and were able to share contacts with a view to working together in the future.

Spring had sprung and our next Saturday evening UNITE event in 2018 was due. The meeting was to be held on 19th May at New Hall Christian Mission in Normacot, just outside Longton. This was the home of the Filipino 'Living Word Church' headed up by Pastor Edgar Gapuz. We had made so many friends in this beautiful and welcoming fellowship which had helped us on multiple occasions at UNITE in leading worship by their talented young musicians. The wedding of Prince Harry and Meghan Markle had taken place earlier in St George's Chapel at Windsor Castle. It was a warm and pleasant day and Bishop Michael Curry had lit up Windsor Castle with his 'fiery love' sermon. However, the temperature was also hotting up in Normacot! The spiritual atmosphere in the New Hall Christian Mission was on fire with love, worship and testimony to Jesus' life-changing power. Around 70 Christians of all ages and backgrounds came together to lift up the name of Jesus.

There was some admirable testimony given from the floor including that of Cliff Roberts and also a man he had brought along. The man was Kevin, who had just spent 23 years in prison and in the last week or so committed his life to Jesus. Alec Gapuz, Pastor Edgar's gifted daughter, also gave a short but very encouraging Bible message. The plan was that three ladies would give their 'no holds barred' testimonies! They were Jan Thompson, her friend Nicky Carbin and Vicky Gardner. These were personal and heartrending stories, and it was clear that without Jesus in their lives their outcomes would have been very different. Food prepared by our hosts at the end of the evening was, as usual, absolutely amazing!

We've arrived at the end of this season of 'new pastures' even though there are still fresh venues for UNITE to explore in the next chapter. However, the new pastures will be seen to be far less significant when compared with our encounters with people who have been involved in the occult and with Christians who have seen prophecy marvellously fulfilled.

CHAPTER 10

FROM DARKNESS TO LIGHT!

". . . to open their eyes, so they may turn from darkness to light and from the power of Satan to God. Then they will receive forgiveness for their sins and be given a place among God's people, who are set apart by faith in me."
Acts 26:18

The above scripture is the message the risen and ascended Lord Jesus gave to Saul while he was travelling to Damascus to persecute Christians and see them cruelly executed for their faith. Jesus was telling Saul that He would appoint him as His servant and witness to take the gospel message to the Gentile (non-Jewish) world. Saul was being divinely transferred from a life devoted to persecuting Christians to one of being a persecuted Christian himself! There could be no greater transformation. This was Saul's Damascus Road conversion! God had a plan for this religious bigot. I believe that God has a plan for all of us human beings and that at some point in our lives He calls us to follow Him. *I know the plans I have for you says the Lord . . .* Jeremiah 29:11. Saul's conversion was sudden and dramatic. It was a miracle. I would suggest that all conversions are a miracle, although most are not as sudden and dramatic. We each have an ongoing testimony which is different to anyone else's, and an important part of UNITE is giving Christians a 'PLATFORM' to share that testimony to encourage others. There have been at least 500 individual testimonies since we began these

Saturday night meetings. Several of these have had the effect of speaking to the hearts of non-Christians present and the Holy Spirit has used that simple message about Jesus to convict them of their sins and lack of faith. As a consequence, many have made commitments to follow Jesus.

A few years ago I met up with an old school-friend after more than 50 years. As we sat having lunch together, he told me that he had once travelled the Middle East with a group of Christians and he told his companions that he would not become a Christian unless he was converted on the Damascus road! Travelling the Damascus road in and out of Syria, he experienced no conversion. That was it. Unfortunately, he realised that he had left some valuable equipment back in the hotel in Damascus so he had to leave his friends and return there to collect it. He told me that on his way back, Jesus spoke to him and told him He wanted him as His disciple. Isn't that remarkable? God uses 'any means' to call people to Himself. Usually, though, those means are people like you and me!

This sort of transformation in a person's life is surely one of moving out of darkness into light; out of ignorance into enlightenment; out of sin and rebellion and into God's righteousness and fellowship. We have briefly touched on witchcraft, the service of Satan, in earlier chapters, but we will discover a little more about this supernatural means of causing harm as we move into this last season of our journey – all the way, giving glory to Jesus!

We exited the last chapter with our UNITE event hosted by our Filipino friends in Normacot. That was on 19th May, 2018. The following Saturday, 26th May, we bore witness to the fruit of much prayer which was initiated by Andy Cannon's 'gate-crashing' our UNITE Pastors and Ministry Leaders Breakfast Meeting the previous month. I am so gladly enlightened when my plans are set aside by the Holy Spirit so He can get on with the real business of extending God's Kingdom. At the Breakfast Meeting I had devised an agenda with a strict timetable and then at the last minute Andy came and changed all that and set on fire the hearts of many leaders there. Actually, he didn't take much more than five minutes to do it! As a result, our friend, Pastor Albert Addaio at 'Gracefields Chapel' agreed to let us use his church in the centre of Hanley on this Saturday morning in May to host the leaders and the ones from their churches who wanted to be involved in this evangelistic outreach in Hanley, the 'City Centre.' This was to be an outreach to tell the people in town the good news that Jesus forgives sins, changes lives and delivers men, women, boys and girls from darkness into His marvellous light. Amazingly, 78 Christians turned up. It would have been good if there were 70, the same number that Jesus sent out two by two, but I was very pleased with this! After prayer and much motivation from Andy and his team, we ventured out into Hanley town centre to share the gospel, pray for folks and encourage the Christians we met.

It was a fine sunny morning and God answered prayer. I saw several groups of us 'ordinary' Christians witnessing to and praying for people in the busyness of the day. I saw Andy and some of his team praying for the lame and sick. I saw several Christians encouraged by all this. After about an hour and a half we returned to 'base' in 'Gracefields' where we heard of at least 15 commitments which had been made by people in the town to follow Jesus. Two people, a man and a woman aged around forty, actually came into the church to testify to everyone that they had made a serious decision to turn away from their past lives and come to God; from darkness into light!

Back to the business of UNITE evening meetings now. Evening meetings, morning outreaches, Pastor's Breakfasts; they are all means to one end, and that is 'Connecting and Encouraging Christians and Introducing people to Jesus.' Our UNITE slogan! It was 16th June and our event was to be held for the second time in the beautiful Herbert Minton Building in Stoke, the home of our RCCG Nigerian friends. Bishop James Kotey was staying with Jean and me and it was good that he was able to be our speaker for this event – bringing Ghana and Nigeria together once again! First though there were several passionate testimonies from a number of folks present, particularly one from an interesting lady who testified to having been involved in the occult as a black witch. She related how she had been delivered from the occult by the love of Jesus. This was intriguing and it's difficult to go into all the details here as the testimony was relatively short. However, if you continue reading you will discover more when this same lady gave a fuller account in the following March of how she was transported from darkness to light! Bishop James spoke on the subject of fear; *'You have not been given a spirit of fear, but a Spirit of love, power and a sound mind'.* 2 Timothy 1:7. There was good response at the end of the evening and James prayed for a number of folks. This church, being in the centre of Stoke, attracts many homeless people, and ours being an open meeting, two homeless men came in at the end. They were given clothing and train fare – and, of course, the gospel.

We had some good times during the summer of 2018 keeping July and August free of UNITE evening meetings. One of them was driving up to St Helens to join Andy and Jen Cannon as Andy celebrated his 40th birthday at the end of July! His home and garden were full of guests, and food, fun and fellowship were flowing. Two days later, Hollybush Christian Fellowship had a true

'Jubilee' celebration of their own as they celebrated their 50th Family Camp Meeting. Jean and I joined them half way through their week. Pastors Jim and Cynthia Wilkinson each heard the audible voice of God tell them he wanted the farm for His glory. The rest is history!

Jean had been wanting us to have a break during the summer of 2018. We had been pushing forward with UNITE events each month and sometimes twice a month. Actually, Jean had booked us on a two week cruise in August! However, before then we fitted in Saturday morning evangelism in the various towns, running a weekly church meeting, church anniversaries, meetings with potential speakers (e.g. the Choi family and Aimee Scoffins), the odd speaking engagement and, of course our annual visit to the Hollybush Family Camp. On 18th August, 2018 Jean and I set of for Southampton to board the 'Britannia' which was to take us to the Mediterranean via Alicante, Barcelona, Monte Carlo, Pisa, Cartagena and Gibralta. There was no church on board ship so we held our own. We met a couple during dinner one evening; they were sitting on the next table to us. We always give thanks to God for our food wherever we are. When this couple, who were our age and from similar backgrounds, saw us praying in the restaurant, they asked us if we were Christians. We told them we were. Then they told us they were Christians too and that they wanted to join us in prayer before each meal for the remainder of the cruise. Previously we hadn't witnessed them praying. I find it disheartening that Christians should feel in any way embarrassed about praying in public. As I recall, on an earlier occasion on a larger dinner table with several others we prayed and most of them joined in.

Returning home on 2nd September, there was much preparation to be made for our 90th UNITE event (also its 7th birthday!) which we had decided to hold in the 'Valiant Suite' at Port Vale Football Club. This was to be a widely circulated event with guests Daniel and Tanya Chand. However, before this there was to be an important and long-awaited presentation made to Jean. For twelve months she had been studying at Pastor Carl and Mandy Scott's Grace and Faith Victory Church in Kidsgrove. On Saturday 8th September Jean was presented with her 'Discipling the Nations' (DtN) certificate in Biblical Studies at Victory Church in Rugeley. I was very proud of her. I must not omit the fact that the following day was mine and Jean's eighteenth wedding anniversary! To celebrate we went to our own fellowship, 'Life Stream Church' to worship God in the morning, had a meal at 'Miller and Carter' afterwards and then returned to 'Life Stream' to witness a baptismal service in the evening. Following various local meetings through that week, we were to see Daniel and Tanya; but this was not to be at UNITE. On 15th September we drove south to Bedford where they live, and booked in to the stately Swan Hotel on the edge of the River (Great) Ouse in the town centre. Yes, there were swans on the river!

Actually I am familiar with this part of the country as relatives on my mother's side live nearby. As a boy I spent many happy summer holidays in this beautiful part of England, many of them fishing in the Great Ouse. On this particular evening, Daniel and Tanya were holding #bedfordRevival18 in the Corn Exchange building a short distance from our hotel and we wanted to surprise them. It was an inspiring event with around 300 folks cramming in to the prestigious edifice. Many decisions for salvation in Jesus were made. The following morning we took a slight detour to St Neots across the border into Cambridgeshire to visit my Aunty Eileen. It was a lovely reunion as Jean and I hadn't seen her for a number of years.

The run-up to our Port Vale event was also a busy one. I was taking a lot on and this was the subject of Steve Moss's counselling me earlier in the year at St Anne's. I guess I knew I should take some sort of break, but somehow as each month arrived, there were speakers/evangelists lined up to minister at our UNITE meetings and we just pressed on.

Finally 22nd September arrived and there we were setting up in the 'Valiant Suite'; we were Port Vale fans again! We had been asked by a local pastor to publicise the need for Christian foster parents in Stoke-on-Trent. It was almost as though I didn't need to say anything. Following the brilliant praise and worship led by Adam Elkington and family, people began coming to the front giving testimonies about fostering or that they had been fostered themselves. It wasn't until after the meeting had ended that I spotted a large banner in the foyer of the Port Vale entrance which was promoting foster care! But all this took place before Daniel and Tanya arrived. They arrived during the interval, so they had no idea what had been said during the 'first half.' The following paragraph is adapted from a newspaper report I had published the following week.

Port Vale was the place to be for good news on Saturday! The 'Valiants' won their away-match with Crewe and many Christians proclaimed the good news of salvation through Jesus Christ as they shared their testimonies. Guest speakers Daniel and Tanya Chand had been ministering at a Wolverhampton conference and arrived late. Before they arrived, a number of Christian foster parents, together with children who were being fostered and adults who had been fostered spoke of their relationship with Jesus and how He had changed the course of their lives and given them new hope. Their appeal was "We need more Christian foster parents!" This was significant as the theme of God's Fatherhood had taken hold of the meeting; the opening song was 'You're a good, good, Father'. When Tanya gave her own testimony she told how she had been fostered following her near death after a suicide attempt aged 13. She was later adopted by her Christian foster parents. She shared how she later accepted Jesus into her heart and the dramatic change which came about in her life. Daniel ministered towards the end of the evening, and an eleven year old girl who was being fostered by one of the audience committed her life to Jesus and was filled with the Holy Spirit; a genuine manifestation of the Holy Spirit's power. Daniel prophesied over her that she would become a powerful evangelist herself. Several others made similar commitments including a young Muslim man. Tanya had simply repeated what she had not heard said before the interval! "We need more Christian foster parents." Right people, right place, right time – Holy Spirit activity as God's people came together in unity!

As I look through Jean's diary at the following four weeks, I can hardly believe the activity and number of meetings we were involved in. One event worth mentioning is the 'Festival of Hope' meeting of the Billy Graham Evangelical Association in the Blackpool Winter Gardens. On the day following our Port Vale UNITE event, we drove up to Blackpool to celebrate Jesus and join 3,000 people as Franklin Graham shared the pure gospel of love and sacrifice of Jesus to save sinners. In the event, we saw around 100 folks make decisions to follow the Saviour.

As time flew by, 20th October rolled round and we were holding UNITE in a new venue for us, Temple Street Methodist Church Hall in Fenton. I had wanted to give our friend Cliff Roberts the opportunity to speak about how the Lord Jesus had turned round the life of an unruly 'ruffy tuffy' lorry driver to a compassionate and considerate friend of society's most unfortunate people, the homeless. Cliff was our main speaker.

The hall was full but the atmosphere intimate at this event. I had had an extremely stressful day dealing with a close relative who had been the victim of a theft some distance away. She couldn't cope with the incident and it was suggested hospital care was necessary. She was on the phone in tears just before the meeting began. I was very upset. The enemy's best tactic! This, or something very similar, has happened on several occasions previously just before UNITE meetings were due to begin. Cliff suggested I could cancel the meeting and offered to drive me the 120 mile return journey to bring my relative back to Stoke-on-Trent. However, my service and promise to God is to hold up this 'platform' (UNITE) He has given me to allow Jesus 'centre stage'. We prayed and pressed on with the meeting. Steve Dailly led worship sensitively as we welcomed Jesus into our presence. Several testimonies came from the floor including one from Kevin Williams who had spent 23 years in prison. He eventually found Jesus to be the one who really cared for him. Also Shaun Wall who had featured in the Sentinel a few days previously told us something about his life. Shaun had been homeless in London and eventually came to S-o-T where he found help and encouragement at Temple Street Church. This church is the 'home' of our friends Glenn and Jacky Parkes who have always been such a help and encouragement to us too. Now Shaun, in turn, gives help and encouragement to the homeless and needy in the city. The love of Christ compels him. In the middle of the testimonies in the 'first half', Sharon Jesse, who goes to the nearby Triumphant Christ Chapel just down the road, got up and began to sing and prophesy, and folks just kept coming out for prayer and ministry. This was a true Holy Spirit 'intervention'; we just continued spontaneously praising Jesus.

In the 'second half' we heard from our friend Cliff Roberts; his testimony of being healed by a Jesus he didn't know, then of committing his life to Jesus. Cliff openly confessed that although he had been a thief, a liar and an adulterer himself, he despised the homeless, the drug addicts and the alcoholics – until Jesus changed him totally. Now Cliff spends his total time, energy and resources together with wife, Lottie and his team at ROTA (Reaching Out To All) helping the homeless, the drug addicts, the down-and-outs and alcoholics in our city! This must be a divine exchange of darkness for light! Cliff is a 'Gideon' Bible distributor, and at the end of the meeting a seven year old boy asked him for two Bibles!

Three weeks later, as the autumn leaves of red and gold drifted by our window, we prepared to stage a UNITE event in Longton Elim Church where our friends Pastors Paul and Lynne Dunne would host us. This was 10th November 2018. Not too many folks came along on the night, perhaps around 40. I was surprised as our main guest was David L'Herroux, the Chief Executive officer at United Christian Broadcasters (UCB); he is an inspired and powerful speaker. Our worship leader for the evening was singer/songwriter Rebecca Proffitt who led sensitively and beautifully. We also had a UCB presentation of their prodigious media resources. Pastor Jon Mason of Stoke's Park Church came to the meeting which really pleased me. I had been trying for some time to encourage the Evangelical churches to be represented at our events. Our faithful follower, Malc Grey-Smart was also there. He always encourages me.

Some truly incredible testimonies followed spontaneously from the floor. Two particularly powerful accounts of God's providence came from a local man called Tony and a young woman called Danielle from N Ireland. On a lighter note, I was able to introduce David L'Herroux by singing a Christian chorus in French! David's theme, which he said God had given him, was 'From Bitter to Sweet.' Using the Israelite's journey into the desert and finding bitter water before God had Moses throw a tree branch into it and it became sweet, David spoke of the bitter times in our lives and how God already had the answer. The sweeter times were there waiting for us if we would truly trust Him. Bitter to sweet; darkness to light! Many went out for prayer at the end of the meeting and some people were definitely touched by God. Sue Parsons, who had served many years at Longton Elim Church with her husband Pastor Phil, was one of these.

We always try to do something different in the run up to Christmas and before everyone has nothing but the seasonal festivities on their minds! Jean and I try to make the meeting early in December in order to give me time to garner support for our two January events. 8th December 2018 was no exception. We were once again at the 'Lighthouse Church' in Burslem. Where better to beam light into darkness?!

Once again, there were lower numbers attending; around 65 folks there. Nevertheless, the event was truly blessed, especially as we had purposely put together a programme consisting of very young Christians with a story to tell. I was concerned that we wouldn't have time to 'squeeze in' the four young people, let alone give opportunity for others there to share a testimony of what the Lord Jesus had been doing. I couldn't resist a little vocal gymnastics by putting the words of 'O Come all ye Faithful' to the tune 'We Wish you a Merry Christmas'. It works quite well!

Aimee Scoffins shared her testimony first. She was due to work a night shift at 9.30pm later that evening. She told of how, at a UNITE event in Silverdale in March 2016, the speaker, Pastor Will Graham prophesied over her and said she would go by trains and boats and planes into the world to give the gospel message to many.

Aimee had never been out of the UK and was also very, very shy. That all changed when Aimee was placed at Revive Church in Hull on a Bible and Evangelism Course. Aimee has just returned from an amazing evangelistic outreach in MEXICO! She is a totally different person and we are waiting to hear of even greater things the Lord will do in her life.

Jonathan Hallyburton aged 22 years led us in worship to begin the evening and then later shared a gospel message mingled with his testimony. Jonathan is a determined and dedicated young man who wants to use his musical talent to take the gospel of Jesus Christ wherever he can. We had some carols too! The Choi Family sang for us just like they have done in the streets of 100s of towns all over the UK. The daughter of the family, Sarah Choi, explained how over 400 folks had given their lives to Jesus under their street ministry and that many had been prayed for. Lastly Matt Coster shared his testimony and told us of his work in planting a church in Biddulph; Lord Street Evangelical Church. From all of these young people we learned so much as they showed a surprising maturity beyond their years. We had some other testimonies from the floor including Tom O'Brien who was currently being sued by a patient whom he brought to a UNITE event once some years before. It was good to see Tom and find him in good spirits. He is a good man. Four pastors were present whom I had never met before. These were good connections and would be included in the invitations for our next Pastors Breakfast Meeting! Another pastor there was Charles Machin. We'd been out in the town with him that morning preaching the gospel. Another was Allan Hayles, pastor of New Testament Church of God in Hanley. This was his first UNITE meeting. At the end of the evening, Cliff Roberts' comment was that this was the best UNITE event ever!

By the beginning of 2019 we had firmly established our January UNITE events in Lytham St Anne's and Biddulph Town Hall as annual traditions. On Thursday 9th January together with Joan Adams and Margaret Cooper, we headed north once again to the Glendower Hotel, St Anne's, to meet and have fellowship with more Staffordshire and Cheshire Christians. We then had a few days to settle in before we joined ranks with the Blackpool and St Anne's folks on the Saturday. All went well and it was great to see our guest, Ellie Palma-Cass once again and have a catch-up. Here is a resume of an email I sent to the Fylde Coast local churches after the UNITE event:

Thank you all for your help in making the UNITE Christian gathering a success and a pleasing offering to God. Around 100 folks came along, most of them from the Blackpool and St Anne's area. Many shared their personal testimonies which really encouraged us to understand how faithful our God is. Pastor Steve Moss and the band from Fylde Christian Service Church led worship in a lively and beautiful way. We had a presentation from Reuben Morley of BGEA recapping some of the hundreds of amazing and life-changing decisions for Christ which came out of the 'Festival of Hope' at Blackpool in September. Our guest speaker, Ellie Palma-Cass was totally 'on fire' for Jesus, she was everything we put on our poster: **"Ellie is a much sought-after Christian inspirational speaker with a testimony described as 'compelling, heart-rending, moving and fascinating'. Her raw energy and sense of fun is driven by a heart that beats for Christ."** *Many lives were touched and truly encouraged by her testimony and the teaching which she skilfully wove into it. So thank you again for displaying the posters, encouraging your folks to come along and putting up with my emails! It isn't easy to put on events so far from home and* *those of you who have helped are really appreciated. I hope you will be able to help next January when the event will be on 11th. May God bless you, your families and your ministries!*

This was an understatement really. Ellie got straight into the hearts of the people; hers was a Holy Spirit discernment of their needs. She is an extremely gifted communicator. Our own Stoke-on-Trent ladies, Rose Smith and Debbie Barlow gave some amazing testimony. In Debbie's case it was God leading her to her lost purse the previous day in Blackpool. Ellie's friend, Debbie McNeill also testified and so did our stalwart friend, Peter Cunningham. His testimony blew me away and he wasn't even going to give it! He had intervened in a street domestic where a woman was being beaten by her partner. Even with a violent background to his name, Peter, because of his Christian obedience, did not retaliate and the shamed man walked off. Peter suffered a few bruises, but he did not stoop to the other man's level! This impressed me so much; I was moved. Two weeks later, Ellie posted on Facebook that eight people who had been in the meeting had reported back claiming healing following prayer. Jean and I were so pleased with the whole weekend; we had seen God move and the numbers were gradually increasing too! It was Steve Moss's birthday so I sung him an appropriate song! I usually put Christian words to secular songs, but on this occasion I sung 'Happy Birthday to You' to the tune of the chorus, 'The Joy of the Lord is Your Strength'.

This January we didn't hold the Biddulph Town Hall event until 26th. This gave me a little more time to circulate it and get the Biddulph churches involved in our first local event of 2019. On the night, around 150 folks from around the Midlands packed the Town Hall to celebrate their faith in Jesus. Back in early 2017 you may recall our guest speaker being former Conservative MP Jonathan

Aitken. Well, to 'balance the books' I decided to ask Rob Flello, former Labour MP for Stoke South to be our guest. Rob spoke with great insight sharing how his faith affected his life as a politician. He told how, as a young man, he would take every opportunity to lampoon Christians. He entered Parliament with the same attitude. It was during his time in Parliament that he began thinking about the deep questions in life; what happens when we die, are we really making the right decisions about people's lives, is it true that Jesus, the Son of God, really did die to pay for our sins? Mr Flello shared how he came through a period of personal doubt with the answers to these questions. The result was that he committed his life to Jesus. From opposition in the darkness to the light of understanding! He spoke very personally and openly about his time in Parliament and the events which led to his conversion.

Following the interval, one of our Pastors from 'Life Stream Church', Liz Holdcroft, announced the opening of 'Transformation Bible School' at the church. Georgina Coster, a nurse, also from Knyperley, spoke about an initiative within the NHS called Christian Medical Fellowship which exists to encourage Christians in their faith at work. Then the floor was open to those present to share what Jesus had done in their lives. Many did so and this really encouraged everyone. One young lady who had only recently become a Christian shared her story and it was impossible to deny the joy which she radiated. Others testified of healing and breaking of addictions through prayer and faith in Jesus. It was a good night.

A little earlier in the month Pastor Jim Wilkinson of Hollybush Christian Centre, aka 'Miracle Valley', asked us to put on UNITE within their Friday evening meeting. So we headed up north on 15th February to join with their meeting that evening. We are usually asked to go around Easter time to avoid the bad weather;

'The North wind doth blow and we shall have snow!' However the weather was fine! The fellowship, praise, worship and atmosphere at Hollybush is totally unique; some would say a little outdated, but what it lacks in trendiness it more than makes up for in Holy Spirit zeal, joy and fervent praise. There is always a sense of God's presence. Furthermore, Pastor Jim, by this time approaching 90 years of age, is always motivated to encourage young men and women in their service for Jesus – I don't mean Jean and me! We had young Yorkshireman Luke Vardy as our speaker last year and this time we had even younger Liverpudlian, Reuben Morley. We have known Reuben a while through his work for the Billy Graham Evangelical Association (BGEA). Following some excellent testimonies from the floor. Reuben lit up the place with his testimony and message; so much so that Joanna (Wilkinson) and some of the leaders asked for him to speak there again. So we made a good link there with Reuben (CONNECTING). He also gave a resume presentation of the 'Lancashire Churches Together' event with Franklin Graham in Blackpool last September; the one Jean and I went to.

We had arranged to hold another UNITE event two weeks later in February 2019 with 'ACE' (aka Warren Furman) from the famous Gladiators TV show. However, at the last minute we had to rearrange this as Warren had double-booked an opportunity of speaking in Rio de Janeiro that weekend! However, before I knew about Warren's Rio trip, Jonathan Cairns asked me if he could come over from Northern Ireland to take part in meetings on the weekend of 1st-3rd March. This was a bit of extra activity I felt I could have done without. I would have to arrange venues and churches who would have Jonathan to help support him for the weekend. I held back in contacting potential host pastors and even planning a UNITE event.

I prayed about this, and I asked the Lord what to do. I felt led to contact two churches and if they said "Yes, we'll have him", I would then arrange a UNITE meeting at short notice and put on the full weekend around it for Jonathan. So that's just what I did. I phoned Pastor Trevor Nicklin at Hanley Baptist Church to ask if he would have Jonathan speak on the Sunday morning. His reply was simply "Yes, that's fine". When I then spoke to Pastor Edwin Cotter at Silverdale Elim Church, he replied "Yes, we'll have him on the Sunday evening and we'll arrange for him, his wife and baby daughter to stay with one of our folks in Madeley". It was then left for me to organise a UNITE event on Saturday 2nd March. With very little notice, our friend Glenn Parkes allowed us the use of the hall at Temple Street Methodist Church and I put out all the advertising. Very soon 2nd March arrived!

I was confident that this event was one 'endorsed' by the Holy Spirit and very soon this became quite obvious. Jean and I knew Jonathan quite well from meeting and hearing him many times at the annual Hollybush Family Camp. But on this evening in Fenton he excelled in preaching the gospel, singing beautifully and testifying. He was a great encouragement! Only a few weeks previously, his wife Tanita, had given birth to their stillborn baby. This tragedy had been playing out through the weeks I was prevaricating over Jonathan's visit. But here they both were with their little girl, Portia, and Jonathan gave a brave and faithful testimony to the goodness of God throughout. If anyone thinks the circumstances do not warrant this statement, please read on to the end of the book and you will find the most remarkable revelation or prophecy over Jonathan and Tanita's life. What a testimony! It was on the next evening at Silverdale Elim that I invited Jonathan to be our speaker at the St Anne's UNITE event in the following January of 2020.

Jonathan's ministry was interspersed with testimony from the 85 folks present. A lady called Deborah Hawkins had previously contacted me about giving her testimony, a song and reading from her book during this meeting. She did just that and did it excellently. This was an amazing story of childhood abuse, drugs and dabbling in the occult leading to satanic activity and witchcraft. Then Jesus delivered her from being a 'black witch' to coming to know Him. This sort of testimony is precious and not readily heard in most churches. A surprise to us was Jane who came with Malcolm and Steph from Market Drayton. She had a background of frustration and sexual promiscuity and had become a 'white witch'. Witches galore! She told her story of being delivered and becoming a Christian. Hallelujah! She also sang her song!

Other worthy testimonies came from Barbara Doughty and Dave Scoffins. When people are possessed by evil spirits, it is truly a remarkable thing that they should be delivered out of the hand of the devil by the blood of the risen Lord Jesus! Of course, there are many who will not accept that any of this can be true, but on this evening, at this UNITE event we all witnessed the truth of two completely different people being taken out of darkness into God's marvellous light! Just as an add-on, I have an excellent book written by a former witch, Doreen Irvine, entitled 'From Witchcraft to Christ'. She came to Stoke-on-Trent in the 90s, I think, and made quite an impression. The book is well worth a read.

A smaller number of around 60 came along to our UNITE event on 23rd March, 2019 which we held in Gracefields Chapel in Hanley. Once again, this was a truly Holy Spirit directed evening and God had some plans to reveal Himself through the testimony and worship. Praise music was led by Rhoda from Gracefields and Sharon Jesse (remember her from our March 2018 event in Temple

Street?), plus Ernest and the drummer both from the church. It was loud and enthusiastic! There were great testimonies from Kevin Williams, Rhys Perinton, Beat Mueller and others. Beat somehow brought in a Hong Kongese lady who spoke only Chinese! She wanted to sing a song in Chinese. Before I knew it she was singing this song! Aimee and Beat were able to communicate and discover from the translation app on their phones that the lady was seeking something and had an awareness of what the meeting was about. Anyway, she went to Gracefields Chapel the following morning.

Luke and Nicola Vardy were our speakers. Nicola gave a long and heart-rending testimony of her life and how she came to know Jesus. There is much more to it than she gave on the evening, but Nicola has since written a book called 'Unbroken: A True Story of a Courageous Young Woman's Journey'; it's available on Amazon. Following this, Luke spoke on John 3:16; a very passionate, very strong and spiritually energetic word. One young lady who came from Leek gave her life to Jesus at the end of Luke's message. She was to feature in our next UNITE event at the Bridge Centre when she announced the date of her baptism. One man called David was healed of deafness and Dave Scoffins claimed to be healed of his arthritis and marched round the room! It was so good to have our friends Luke and Nicola stay with us overnight and catch up on Kingdom news! Luke spoke at 'Life Stream' the following morning; healings and one Salvation took place.

Before we leave this season of 'From Darkness to Light' let me say that we believe in the absolute inerrancy of the scriptures and their Holy Spirit inspiration. Jesus said *"I am the light of the world"*, He also said *"You are the light of the world"*. So here are two equivalent scriptures for us to ponder.

The light shines in the darkness, and the darkness can never extinguish it. John 1:5

The path of the righteous is like the morning sun, shining ever brighter till the full light of day. Proverbs 4:18

Jesus came into the world to bring the light of God's Kingdom to men and women. As the sun's light is reflected by the moon, so should Jesus's light be reflected by His true followers; you and me. He shines that light on us, and the closer our relationship to Him, the more we will shine for Him. At UNITE meetings I have often sung the song *'This little light of mine, I'm gonna let it shine.'* Jesus requires us to bring the light of the gospel to people in darkness. This means telling them that God loves them and that Jesus died for them to set them free; He rose from death and He is alive today and He's calling them to repent, believe and receive eternal life in His name. We also believe that at UNITE, when we meet together in unity on these matters, we are in accord with Him and the Holy Spirit is pleased to offer salvation. We have seen this so many times and I am sure there are many instances of people being touched by the Holy Spirit in ways that we may never hear about. But let's get out of any darkness we've mentioned and reflect on the beauty of the light, but let us also allow that light to be reflected by those of us who are trusting in Jesus for our salvation and following him daily.

It's time to take a last 'breather', reflecting on what has passed and looking ahead to what came next between the months of April 2019 and February 2020. Just a 'mixed bag' of UNITE events and occurrences to bring us to a conclusion – for the time being! Subjects that come to mind are 'Centenary', 'Special Anniversary', 'A Tamed Villain', more salvations, a hernia operation and LOCKDOWN!

CHAPTER 11

DIVERSITY

God's purpose is now to show the rulers and powers in the heavens the many different varieties of his wisdom through the church.
Ephesians 3:10

I looked up the definition of diversity and found it to mean 'a varied mixture'. There is plenty of variety in this final chapter where we will read of new venues, old venues, new speakers, familiar speakers, a bit of adventure, some breakthrough, a double celebration, end-of-life Salvation, God's healing in the hands of a surgeon and, as a climax, some of the most compassionate and Spirit-guided ministry I have ever witnessed. Through this diversity runs a theme. The theme is unity. *Make every effort to keep the unity of the Spirit through the bond of peace.* Ephesians 4:3

So we have made it to the final lap of the journey so far! It's 2019 and to begin this part of our excursion we decided to hold our 27th April UNITE event, once again, in the spacious Bridge Centre in Birches Head near Hanley. You may remember our 'Jubilee' chapter when we celebrated our 50th UNITE meeting. We were now about to celebrate our 'double Jubilee', our 100th Saturday evening event; our Centenary! I've quoted the headline from my newspaper report of this meeting: *While storm Hannah was giving North Staffordshire a soaking at the weekend, inside the Bridge Centre in Birches Head, Jesus was reigning! A large crowd of worshippers came to help celebrate Christian group Unite's 100th Saturday evening event.* We had arranged for Evangelist, and by now our old friend, Andy Cannon to speak (actually he insisted!), we had a gifted worship band come all the way from Liverpool and many Christians, new and old, came along to join in the celebrations. I should add that we really came to celebrate Jesus who made all this possible! We decked out this main auditorium with balloons in the shape of 100 and with other trimmings; the food during the interval was sumptuous.

The 'first half' got underway with some quite intense praise and worship music. This was followed by testimonies from a number of folks who had never been to a UNITE event before. The young woman from Leek who committed her life to Jesus at our last event gave a shout 'I'm getting baptised tomorrow'. This was good news because I am eager to see new believers carry on their Christian journey with the Lord. However, this was to be a bitter sweet experience for us all. More about this later in the chapter. However, I would really like to draw your attention to one young man who had also been to a UNITE event previously – but not for almost eight years. Let me tantalise you a little longer. He established and leads a dynamic youth group in Lancashire and had travelled the 60 miles from Blackburn with his dad to be at this meeting. You will not have guessed who it is, but if you were to refer to the end of Chapter 1, you would find the name of an eight year old boy who committed his life to Jesus at our very first UNITE event. It was, of course Micah Boulton, now almost sixteen years old. Micah had been baptised a few years back and his testimony was like a beacon shining into the hearts of many followers of Jesus in the Bridge Centre, encouraging them and making them aware that there are young folks in our nation on fire for the Saviour. I did a little dictionary reseach. The name Micah means *Who is like God?* and the definition of beacon is: *a fire or light set up in a high or prominent position as a celebration!* Micah's testimony was passionate and appropriate.

Andrew Cannon was full of enthusiasm and fire for the Lord Jesus, as he always is. He encouraged those present to make use of their God-given gifts to change the spiritual atmosphere around them. He urged them to use love and care to share the Gospel of Jesus Christ with those whom they meet. Many folks went out for prayer at the end of the evening and received ministry and prayer. Just looking through my diary, Andy spoke at Alsager Community Church the following morning when a young man committed his life to Jesus.

That was our 100th UNITE event, it was a momentous landmark for us. I just checked Chapter 1, and in the first paragraph I saw that I'd written about the first event: *'we didn't know if anyone would turn up'!* We had moved on considerably since then, but if we felt we could sit back and take it easy, we were wrong. It seemed that a great momentum was building with every meeting. UNITE had begun as a Saturday evening Christian event back in 2011. A few years later we began gathering Christians together on Saturday mornings to take out the gospel to folks on the streets, speaking to individuals, praying with them and leading them to Jesus. We met some really gifted Christians who responded to our appeals for them to join our little UNITE team and we discovered that many of these evangelists (because that is what they are) found it quite natural to lead strangers to Jesus. Once again, following prayer, Jean and I simply provided the 'platform'. We did this many times in all the six Potteries Towns and if I could include the surrounding towns of Congleton, Kidsgrove, Alsager and Newcastle (making ten towns), we could identify with Jesus's travels: *Then Jesus left the vicinity of Tyre and went through Sidon, down to the Sea of Galilee and into the region of the Decapolis (The Ten Towns)!* Mark 7:31! Furthermore, in 2018, after much prayer, Jean and I began a series of Pastors' and Ministry Leaders' Breakfast Meetings. I mentioned some of these previously and the fruit of these meetings has been remarkable. So we really were diversifying!

Now it is time to move on, let's diversify further! For some years I had wanted to mark the anniversary of the famous and very significant Camp Meeting on Mow Cop which took place on 31st May, 1807. I mentioned this early in Chapter 6 when we held our 'Jubilee' UNITE event in 2015. This was a very significant outdoor meeting of Christians who had been rejected by the Methodist Church of the day. They preached, prayed and saw many, many local folks come to a saving knowledge of Jesus. According to John Walford, Hugh Bourne's biographer, this *promoted one of the greatest revivals of the religion of Jesus Christ among the labouring masses that was ever known in the British Isles;* the Primitive Methodist Revival. I mention it again as my 3xgreat grandad, Sam Barber of Tunstall, was the first black preacher in this move of God. He was there at the beginning with the great men, Hugh Bourne and William Clowes, and later, when the 'breakaway' Primitive Methodist Church was established, as a preacher, member of the first Church Council and the secretary of the 'New Testament and Religious Tract Society'. That's my 3xgreat grandad, and I'm very much in awe of him. Knowing him as my forebear has been a great inspiration and encouragement and has motivated me to begin these UNITE events and to continue with them for all these years. I would also add that finding out about him has been perhaps one of the most significant discoveries of my life next to coming to know Jesus as my Saviour – but what could be more significant than that?!

Here is a short SELAH interlude. You may remember the young lady who committed her life to Jesus in our March meeting under Like Vardy's ministry. At our 100th event in April she shouted out that she would be getting baptised the following day at her church in Leek. Thanks to a lady named Annette telling her about Jesus, she had believed in Him as her Lord and Saviour and was baptised. She was saved! We heard the sad news a few weeks later that after she failed to obtain the help she needed for her mental problems she had passed away. I would prefer to say she had gone to be with Jesus in glory; the certainty of every born-again believer.

Camp Meeting anniversary day, 31st May arrived. However, we did not hold our UNITE event on this day! We decided to have it on the following day, 1st June, as this was a Saturday when I felt it would be better attended. I was still conscious of numbers attending! I'm not aware of any newspaper report in the nearby towns of Congleton and Biddulph from 1807, but here is an extract from a report I had published in the 'Biddulph and Congleton Chronicles' of our UNITE celebration of the 212th anniversary!

Way back in 1807, on May 31st, thousands gathered at Mow Cop for what was called a 'Camp Meeting'. It was a significant Christian event and it kick-started a spiritual revival and social change which revolutionised our area. This was the 'Primitive Methodist Revival'. Last Saturday, local Christian group, 'Unite' celebrated the anniversary, appropriately, in the Mow Cop Primitive Methodist Church in Primitive Street when over 100 folks joined together to give Jesus first place and to worship God. Several gave their Christian testimonies. One of these was a young man with a background of prison, violence and drugs who turned his back on all those things and committed his life to Jesus just over a year ago. He announced he was to be baptised the following day. Guest speaker was Simon Edwards. Simon's past was one of extreme abuse as a child, gang violence, enforcing and armed robbery. He was sentenced to life imprisonment. It was while he was in Dovegate Prison that he met with Jesus who transformed his life. Six years ago, Simon was released and has tirelessly worked to help rehabilitate ex-offenders on leaving prison. He set up 'WALK Ministries in Tunstall which gives men coming out of prison an opportunity of a home, a job, a church and a new start in life. The young man previously mentioned was helped in this way by 'WALK'. Some of the old hymns were sung in a new way as Jonathan Hallyburton from Congleton led worship. Here our new friend, Apostle Dancho Asenov from Bulgaria, gave some testimony about his Christian work in many Eastern European Countries to bring Christian 'UNITY to the Nations'!

Not only did we celebrate a significant historical event, but we also did something quite innovative ourselves. Mow Cop Primitive Methodist Church, which is built on the site of the original Camp Meeting, is a beautiful and well-preserved old building. Our friend, Kacey Scullion, has worked hard to keep the fellowship interested and involved in the local community. However, their congregation, like those of many rural Methodist Churches, is small. It was heartening to see over 100 folks come to this UNITE event and even more so to have Anglican, Methodist, Evangelical and Pentecostal ministers take part. It was a very lively event to say the least! Testimonies were radical and passionate. The music for our praise and worship was brilliantly delivered by Jonathan Hallyburton who had participated in our UNITE event just before Christmas. Simon

Edwards was truly on form speaking from the heart about his relationship with his Saviour and 'telling it like it is'!

Although our next event on 29th June, 2019 was also in a Methodist Church, there were a few things about it which were novel. Our speaker was Chris Jones from Nottingham and I had never met him. Chris had phoned us a few times over the years from the New Life Newspaper publishers where we ordered newspapers to take out round our estate. He helped New Life with telesales. One time, not long before this UNITE event, I spoke to Chris about Jesus and he told me the remarkable account of his own conversion. I knew we would have to have him speak at UNITE. Newchapel Methodist Chapel is the place where Jean's family attended and where she went to Sunday School. My mum, 94 years of age at the time of this event, was also a regular attender there. It's fair to say that we have good connections with the chapel but although it's only a short distance from our home, I would never have considered holding a UNITE event there. It was attended by only about six folks and there was talk of its closing. Some months previously, I was able to help Pastors Carl and Mandy Scott secure the rental of the building for their own Grace and Faith Victory Church meetings when they found themselves needing new premises. This helped liven things up a little in Newchapel and it was a joy to witness the unity when the two churches united together for a Christmas service later that year.

The relatively small chapel was filled, folks travelling from Birmingham and Nottingham, and an air of excitement buzzed through the building. Testimonies flowed giving honour and praise to Jesus our mighty Saviour. We felt the theme 'God has a plan for your life' was being brought out by the Holy Spirit through these testimonies. Chris Jones gave an account of his life and how, after a difficult childhood in several foster homes, he turned to petty crime. At age 19 and disillusioned with crime, Chris told how he began researching various religions. He found that none of them gave him the answers he was looking for. So he returned to crime! After an extraordinary turn of events, Chris found himself committing his life to Jesus. He shared his evidence and experience to show that the Christian faith is reason-based and real. Carl and Mandy led us in some truly inspired praise and worship and Jean provided an appetising buffet table for the interval.

It was now late summer 2019 and at this time in the calendar we had become accustomed to hosting Daniel and Tanya Chand. This year was no exception. I have come to regard these events with Daniel as very special anointed occasions but, although I advertised the event well, only around 100 folks came along. Jean would tell me that didn't matter! There was lots of Christian testimony, much of it drawing attention to the compassion shown by local Christians to people in need in our area, and also of the Gospel of Jesus Christ which is being shared more and more on our streets. This was good news as Daniel and Tanya spend much of their time giving out the Gospel of Jesus Christ on the streets of our large cities. A man who had been through some very difficult times and had suffered an horrendous leg injury and had his leg in a sort of metal brace testified how he had been helped and looked after by Edie Hindmoor at his lowest point. This was no surprise to us as Edie lives out her Christian faith in her B&B in Hanley.

Following Tanya's gripping testimony, Daniel, our main speaker, told of the centrality of Jesus in dramatically transforming his life and the lives of thousands he has ministered to. Many were prayed for at the end of the meeting and people with sicknesses were healed, some committed their lives to Jesus and many were called upon to be baptised in the Holy Spirit. A close friend of ours had brought her daughter to the meeting and she committed her life to Jesus. Interestingly, our friend's husband had also committed his life to Jesus at a UNITE event a few years previously. She was thrilled!! Another friend told us later that a prominent issue which had affected her life was ministered to during the meeting and she later told us of the dramatic effect it has had on her. We can never underestimate the significance of what God has been doing in these meetings where His people meet together in unity. This was the last UNITE event at which Daniel ministered for us. Since then he has gone on to do great evangelical 'exploits' across the UK and beyond. I see Daniel as one of the forerunners in spreading the Good News of Jesus Christ and experiencing revival wherever God sends him in the coming years.

Here's something a little different. You may remember in the last chapter, back in February, we were to have hosted 'ACE' – aka Warren Furman – from the famous Gladiators TV show. However, at the last minute we had to rearrange this as Warren had double-booked an opportunity of speaking in Rio de Janeiro that weekend! Well, on 21st September, 2019 Warren arrived at our house all ready to roll at our UNITE event in the Alsager Civic just over the border in Cheshire. I had tried very hard to attract as many local folks as possible; ones who probably would not have responded if the event were in a church. We had a good number come along, but mostly Christians. Here is an extract from the newspaper report I put in the local Chronicle:

Alsager Civic became an 'arena' for former television Gladiator, 'ACE' on Saturday evening! 'ACE', whose real name is Warren Furman, travelled down from York to talk to a gathered crowd at Christian group, Unite's latest event. He spoke of his celebrity lifestyle, expensive cars, houses and having just about everything he wanted. He said that as the Gladiator show, which attracted 14 million viewers, came to an end he realised that he had been 'living a lie'. Attempting to discover the meaning of life, Warren examined many religions but eventually went to an 'Alpha Course', asked lots of questions over a period of time and discovered a real relationship with God for himself and with that an even more exciting lifestyle too. His fervent desire was that all people should have the opportunity to hear and examine God's message in the Bible and have the opportunity to commit their lives to Jesus and to be filled with the Holy Spirit. Warren has also worked with the Archbishop of York, John Sentamu on Christian missions and visits to prisons. The evening was enjoyed by folks from all over Cheshire and North Staffordshire. The group wishes to thank Pastor Pete Howard and the Alsager Community Church band for hosting them and leading worship during the evening.

We moved into the Community Church next door during the interval for food -excellently prepared by Jean! – and a more intimate atmosphere for a really valuable Question and Answer session which followed. Warren really interacted so well with an engaging gathering of folks. Interspersed with the Q&A session were some lovely testimonies of the goodness of God from several present.

A certain date in my diary was looming! For over a year I had been in great discomfort when standing for long periods of time particularly at UNITE meetings. I was having pain from a hernia and I had arranged to go in for an operation in the Royal Stoke Hospital. The date was arranged at relatively short notice by the hospital for 10th October in this year of 2019. I like to advertise and organise the UNITE events well in advance and, as it happened, I had already arranged to hold our next event on 12th October.

Everything was in place: venue, speakers, band, advertising. I didn't think I would be up to hosting the event and so I arranged for my friend, Pastor Carl Scott to run the meeting through and just simply take my place. On 9th October, the Wednesday before the UNITE event, my operation was cancelled! Carl said he would still stand in for me and for the first time in 105 meetings, I would be able to sit back and enjoy the proceedings. So on the Saturday we set up and waited for folks to come along. As the meeting was in Gateway Church at Leek in the Staffordshire Moorlands, I didn't expect a large crowd, but we did well with a good number turning up. When Carl arrived, he must have seen my excitement for the evening because he suggested I convened it; so I did.

There is a little more background to this particular meeting. As anyone who has been to a few of our UNITE events will know, I am very keen to bring together Christians who love the Lord Jesus, believe His word, the Bible, and seek to obey Him. This identifies the 'whosoever' mentioned many times in the Bible. Of course, there are some who seek to interpret the words of others to mean something contrary to their own tenets of faith and so disagree with them: 'majoring on minors'! No denomination has a monopoly on this! Unfortunately, it has caused division between denominations going back to the Reformation. Fortunately, we don't kill each other anymore because of this, but the lack of 'mingling' and fellowship between the different church 'flavours' in the family of God is a sad symptom. Since Jesus' passion for unity within His church is so great, this doctrinal 'majoring on minors' has become a stumbling block. At UNITE we have tried to reverse this idea that "We're the ones who've got it right, you're the ones who've got it wrong" mentality. We are non-denominational with the ministry of reconciliation! I really feel so much love for the family of God and I long for harmony among its members. The song we sing is well-known to UNITE 'regulars':

The family of God keeps growing
The family of God keeps sowing
The seeds of a new life every day.

You want to know the Saviour, I know how hard you've tried
You've tried your best behaviour and you're still not satisfied
Well come and give your heart to Him, He'll not let you down
He's the Saviour to the sinner and the best friend in town.

The family of God keeps growing
The family of God keeps sowing
The seeds of a new life every day.

This October event was originally scheduled to take place in Park Church, Stoke, an Evangelical church. A pastor there, Jon Mason, is one of a few Evangelical leaders who have come along to our events. It was Jon's father, Howard Mason, the pastor back in 1995, who baptised me! Jon is a friend and a good leader who would also like to see a little more 'blending' in God's family, the Church of the Lord Jesus. To this end we arrived at the point where we were 99% sure that the meeting would be in Park Church. Quite late in the arrangements however, it was not possible to go ahead with the venue. I had particularly chosen as speakers a young missionary couple who were part of an Evangelical Anglican church, St Thomas, in Kidsgrove. I felt they would link up the various denominational predispositions under the banner of missionary evangelism! I do believe God had plans for this particular event and, especially in this case, just as Jean said, He sent along the people He wanted at the new venue which I had hurriedly arranged. It was a Pentecostal church!

The evening began with an extremely lively and Spirit-led time of praise and worship led by the in-house band with Adam Elkington and Becky Zacune. A good crowd of Potteries and Moorland folk listened intently to the story of the adventures of Simeon and Gemma Locke and their young family. The Lockes are missionaries in Mali, N.W. Africa taking the gospel of Jesus to the Suninke tribe. Simeon and Gemma gave an enthusiastically illustrated talk about the challenges and rewards of their work, giving thanks to God for their safety, health and progress in seeing many come to faith in Jesus. They also spoke of their concern for the welfare of the native population, particularly the young. An animated Question and Answer session followed with one 10 year old boy asking "What is your goal?" The reply was simply to see the lives of many Suninke people improved both physically and spiritually. I learned that Timbuktu was in Mali!

There then followed several testimonies from local Christians giving evidence of God's interest in and goodness to people in the area of N. Staffordshire. Cliff Roberts gave some amazing details of his work with the homeless and also his Gideon work. Gary Lovatt also spoke in support of Cliff's work with the homeless. Dave and Annette Barber plus Simeon's mum and dad from St Thomas, Kidsgrove were there to support them and Dave prayed to open the evening. I mention Dave and Annette because we met them at St Thomas and I discovered that Dave's granddad was my grandad's brother, making us second cousins, I think!

Because I was anticipating my operation in October, I arranged no further meetings in 2019. This was partly because I wasn't sure if I would be my usual self but also because after the cancellation I was told to expect another date for the operation any time. Strangely, my diary was still full! It was also time to get started arranging and circulating the first two UNITE events in 2020. Then the message came through. The new date for the operation was 21st November. Everything went smoothly this time and at 6am our friends and UNITE supporters, Peter and Sadie, were waiting outside our home to take me to the Royal Stoke Hospital. I soon found myself in the Lyme Building huddled together with a large group of people all registering for operations. I was in the waiting ward for quite some time even though I was given slot number 2 for the op. However, there was a power cut and all the operations were delayed for a few hours. I was a bit nervous, never having had an operation before, but it gave me the opportunity to speak to others on the ward about my God and what He had been doing in my life. I wasn't allowed to have a drink for around ten hours before going into the operating theatre. That was alright, at least I wouldn't need the 'little boys' room'! It was around 2pm when they cut me open! I was under general anaesthetic and didn't feel a thing. I came round a little while later and all had gone well. Thank you Lord. I was looking forward to going home, but in order to do so I was required to give a urine sample, so I drank lots of water and cups of tea. But for whatever reason, I couldn't give a sample and by 9pm I was told I had to stay overnight. What a night it was; no sleep, in and out of the toilet and bumping into the two other men on the ward who were in doing the same! The following morning the nurse wasn't satisfied with my sample and told me I had to stay in further. I managed to talk my way out of that and by around 11.30am I was home. Our friend Terry Longshaw very kindly drove me from the hospital.

The remainder of the year went quietly, apart from running our Tuesday afternoon church meeting ('Tuesday Venue') some street evangelism – and we had a General Election! Apart from the 'hiccup' of my operation, things were going very well with the UNITE ministry. During the last few months we had held a very well attended Pastors and Ministry Leaders Breakfast Meeting and seen several folks commit their lives to Jesus on the streets and in the meetings. I had already organised a number of ongoing UNITE events and I was very excited about what God was going to do in the New Year.

2020 arrived. I called it the year of 20/20 vision. I hadn't got a clue what the year would bring but I was expecting great things! We had UNITE events booked every month until the end of June with some really good new speakers and special venues lined up. Our first event of the year was our traditional seaside UNITE meeting in the Glendower Hotel in Lytham St Anne's. Once again a really good crowd turned up adding to the number of Stokies attending the event; this was our eighth year in St Anne's. Over a number of years Jean and I had met Jonathan Cairns at the Hollybush Family Camp. Jonathan has been a guest there many times and it was good to meet up with him at Silverdale Elim the previous March to arrange for him to be our speaker/singer at this 2020 St Anne's UNITE event. So this time I was ready for him and expecting great things from the Lord. Once again Steve Moss and the band from Fylde Christian Service Church (FCSC) in St Anne's led worship in their usual very lively and truly inspired manner. What a blessing Steve has been to Jean and me and to all at these events over the years. Jonathan and I agreed to just go with the Holy Spirit flow and so he sang, testified and proclaimed God's word with testimonies from the floor interspersed. Jonathan has an excellent knowledge of some of the old hymns and choruses and he encourages the audience to join in. They don't need much encouraging! The testimonies began with Peter Cunningham. We prayed for the healing of some pain in his forehead. A lady named Ruth spoke of some of her deliverance experiences. Spencer gave one of his poems. An 81 year old man called Gordon from Preston spoke of the goodness of God during his experience of losing his wife. Graham from FCSC spoke of being allowed to set up a healing ministry in France in a Catholic church which wasn't being used. Several more testimonies followed. Jonathan ministered so comfortably around these gripping testimonies. He sang beautifully and some of us joined him in praying for many at the end of the evening. We had begun to discover that the Holy Spirit anointing on these Saturday evening UNITE events remains overnight! It has happened so many times before. The following morning Jonathan faithfully delivered the gospel message of salvation through Jesus Christ at FCSC in St Anne's. We took around 24 of the Stoke-on-Trent folks to FCSC and swelled the congregation; the newly extended church was packed! Five people responded to the Gospel appeal to give their lives to Jesus. We were just so thrilled by the way God blessed us through this wonderful weekend.

Dear reader, if I didn't know you before, I hope by now, I may call you a friend. 'UNITE, the Journey' has covered almost nine years of monthly and sometimes bi-monthly Saturday evening events – with a sprinkling of miscellany along the way for good measure – and we've travelled together through this book! We have reached what I believe is the summit of the journey and I want to give you a report of the last meeting we held before that new word came into our vocabulary: 'LOCKDOWN'! Before I do, however, I will describe a few of the coincidences which Jean calls God-incidences that took place over the preceding seven or eight months leading up to this.

In the summer of 2019, my friend, Rev'd Jeff Short, contacted me to recommend a man with a very chequered background to speak at

UNITE. Jeff produces a mid-day programme for Stoke-on-Trent's 'Cross Rhythms' Christian radio station where he often has guests with out-of-the-ordinary life stories. I rarely have a speaker at UNITE whom I haven't met before and somehow I gave this man no further thought. A few weeks later Jean and I took a few days break in Llandudno. They were the hottest days of the year and one evening we attended a 'Beach Missions' Christian open-air meeting on the seafront. Young people were giving their testimonies and we were singing hymns and choruses and generally having a great time. Sitting next to me was an older lady who was 'full of it'. She was on fire for Jesus, singing with gusto! We struck up a conversation and I realised we had met before, but I couldn't think where. Then it all came back to me. It was a year or so previously in Longton market in Stoke-on-Trent. I had been placing a UNITE poster on the notice board and I helped her to put up one of hers. She was publicising a choir concert at Longton Central Hall Methodist Church where Jeff Short is the minister. She told me on that occasion how much she loved the Lord Jesus. Her name was Doreen Houseman. Jean is often being introduced to ladies I have met in one place or another! Doreen reminded me that Jeff had mentioned the man whom he had interviewed on 'Cross Rhythms'. I tried to store the information in my memory, still not knowing the man's name.

In the following month of August Jean and I made our customary visit to the Hollybush Family Camp. On one of the evenings I sat next to a big man who was bouncing up and down to the unique Hollybush praise experience. He was pushing me around quite a lot as we were cramped into the main auditorium. But we struck up a conversation; he loved the Lord Jesus! He was so full of joy and his face shone. I really felt lifted and encouraged by just being with him. Then at the end of the evening he left. I didn't see him again during the remainder of the camp. I wondered who he was. It was a week or so later when I recognised this man on the Hollybush Facebook page. His name was Allen Langham and he was the man whom Jeff had recommended to me months before. Another 'God-incidence'. I was determined to get this man to UNITE. Then in October we went to the 'One-by-One' Conference at 'Renew Church' in Uttoxeter, the church of Pastors Matt and Becky Murray. We have supported this ministry ('One-by-One') since Matt spoke at one of our UNITE events. Who should be there but Allen Langham! We made the arrangements there and then for him to speak at our February 2020 UNITE event. So that is the lead-in to the final event covered in this book; the last event we put on and probably the most passionate and spiritually productive weekends we've ever had.

29th February 2020 was the date. The place was St Stephen's Church in Bentilee. The event was our 107th Saturday evening UNITE event. Jean and I had visited St Stephen's a few times to take part in their Sunday worship service and get to know a few of the folks there. We don't like to just turn up, put on the meeting and then leave. In fact, we made a few good friends there and in the process they joined us in taking the gospel out into the streets of Hanley and Longton. The vicar at St Stephen's is the amazing Rev'd Dave Street. He was so keen and full of enthusiasm for us to put on this event and he helped us in so many ways. I couldn't visit beforehand as much as I would have liked as I felt so ill with a really bad cough; this lasted for around five weeks. On the night, Storm Jorje was raging in Stoke-on-Trent but, even so, a good crowd turned up for the meeting. We had a powerful time of prayer beforehand, with Dave Street and some of his people joining us together with Malcolm Grey-Smart and Allen Langham plus a good number of others I couldn't see because my eyes were closed! Leaving the prayer room and entering the main hall we encountered that special atmosphere we have experienced so many times before. It was an atmosphere of holy expectation! I recognised quite a few well-known local faces; Lamont Howie (Radio Stoke), Richard Walley, Jeff Short – and my daughter, Caroline who had travelled up from Market Drayton. I also know that there were several people off the very large Bentilee estate who had just come along after being invited or had seen the advertising.

I have purposely omitted the fact that at the beginning of each UNITE event I sing a song. Perhaps most people wished I hadn't! On this occasion the song was:

I saw the light at UNITE when I went to St Stephen's
I was in darkness my life was a mess when I came
He came to meet me
As I received Him He washed me and wiped out my shame

My, my, my, Lord Jesus
Why, why, why, Lord Jesus
So before you come to open the door
Forgive me Lord Jesus I don't want my shame any more.

I was ashamed of the person that I had grown into
I needed a Saviour and Jesus was there all the time
I want to praise you
You are my God and I'll walk with you all of my life

Maybe you will guess the tune was 'Delilah', and all the Stoke fans joined in! We prayed the Lord's Prayer together – it was powerful. Then Rev'd Dave led the band in some real upbeat praise and worship songs. It was cold and stormy outside but the spiritual climate in St Stephen's was rapidly moving up the scale.

I quickly handed over to our guest speaker, Allen Langham. We had given him a big build-up in the Sentinel local newspaper and BBC Radio Stoke. His amazing transformation from pro rugby player, violent hard man, enforcer, organised crime, drink, drugs and prison to a beautiful Christian man with a big heart for the broken was so real. Allen ministered to so many at 'interval time' and there were at least five decisions made by people publicly committing their lives to Jesus. Many were prayed for. It was so encouraging to see so much real response. This created a 'natural interval' for food, drink and fellowship. We resumed in the 'second half' with testimonies from the floor. Linda and Linden Harrison came out and Linda testified to answer to prayer for healing from cancer. Vicky Gardner also testified; once again she was amazing!! This led to an introduction for her with Lamont Howie and a subsequent radio interview where she gave her Christian testimony. (CONNECTIONS!) We then did a Question and Answer session with Allen before ending the evening with a 'bang' (Dave Street's description!) as we sung 'To God be the Glory'. What a tremendously blessed evening!

Allen and his seven year old son, Carson, stayed the night with us. It was good getting to know Allen after knowing about him for so long. Incidentally, if anyone would like to hear more of his story, read his book: 'Taming of a Villain'. It was nominated for the People's Book Prize. Needless to say, we had a late night, but we also had an early morning! This was Sunday 1st March and I had scheduled three meetings into the day for Allen. They were to be at Cheadle New Life Centre at 10.30am, Longton Central Hall 'Gospel Café' at 3pm and Congleton New Life Church 7pm. A man committed his life to Jesus in the morning and many of the most unlikely people were ministered to throughout the day. It was a truly extraordinary day and I am very confident that God's Holy Spirit was touching and changing the lives of so many. We were very fortunate that David Green (Christian Television) was present to professionally film Allen's testimony in the evening. This has been circulated considerably throughout the year. We were tired by the time Allen returned to Doncaster to say the least. Allen must have been exhausted himself. His young son, Carson, who accompanied him, seemed to thrive!

We have come to the end of an era; we have arrived at the end of this part of our journey with UNITE and we have reached the end of this book! Thank you for travelling with us. The ministry opportunities for Jean and me ended on 14th March 2020, fourteen days after the weekend with Allen Langham. We went out on the streets of Hanley with the gospel and a number of people committed their lives to Jesus. The Coronavirus 'Lockdown' came into force on March 23rd and, like many others, we found our lives turned upside down. We have now become accustomed to attending meetings on Zoom, Facebook and YouTube (but not too accustomed!!). However, our God is a great God and He sees the end from the beginning. I believe He still has plans for UNITE and tasks to be accomplished: 'Connecting and Encouraging Christians and Introducing people to Jesus'. The work will go on. Amen!

EPILOGUE

I often wondered why the departure buildings at airports are called 'terminals'. It doesn't sound very reassuring especially for someone making their first plane journey; it sounds rather like the end! But thousands of people queue up there to board their plane without giving it a thought. They are not discouraged, and neither are we simply because we have reached the end of a season of UNITE events. It's NOT terminal! In fact, the last words of this book were 'The work will go on'.

On the one hand, we see Pastor Jim Wilkinson at 90 years of age eagerly looking forward to taking the Hollybush journey into the future; on the other, coming up to 73 years of age, Jean and I wonder how much longer I can continue jumping off stages and singing daft songs! But if the work of providing this 'Platform' is from God, and we truly believe it is, then continue, it will. God certainly 'opened a door' for us to put on the outreach and events of the last nine years. *See, I have set before you an open door, and no one can shut it* . . . Revelation 3:8.

At the time of writing, it is almost twelve months since we had to call a halt to all our UNITE activities. Twelve months since people met together in Jesus' name, hugged each other, prayed and laid hands on sick folks, praised and worshipped God with loud and joyful voices; just simply enjoying great Christian fellowship. Now we are subject to a more severe lockdown than ever to try and break the cycle of infection, but we have a vaccine which the medical experts say will significantly help in bringing Coronavirus to an end. Greater still we have a God who is able to bring plagues to an end through the prayers of His people. However, we are likely to be sampling something of what is yet to come. Once again, greater still is the 'blessed hope' of the born-again Christian, the glorious appearing of our great God and Saviour, Jesus Christ who will return to this earth to put a stop to wars, famines and plagues. So, in the words of Pastor Jim Wilkinson, let's "Cheer up" and use this time to pray, increase our faith and examine and prepare ourselves to serve God in new and higher ways in the time he has given us.

If you have been encouraged or even inspired by this book, we'd love to hear from you because its people like you who have inspired and encouraged people like us! How has Jesus turned your life round? How has He changed your circumstances? Please let us know. If this has not happened for you yet, still let us know and consider praying the prayer on the flyleaf of this book. Furthermore, if you feel led by the Holy Spirit to take up the UNITE baton and hold similar events in your area (even if that's Stoke-on-Trent!), we will encourage and help you all we can. We want to see this important ministry of unity continuing until the Lord Jesus appears in the clouds!

It has been our privilege to have you 'on board'! We love you and we're here to pray for you. Your brother and sister in Jesus Christ, Cedric and Jean Barber

cedricbarber908@gmail.com

A prayer

Dear God in heaven, I come to you in the name of Jesus. I acknowledge to You that I am a sinner, and I am sorry for my sins and the life that I have lived; I need your forgiveness.

I believe that Your unique Son Jesus Christ shed His precious blood on the cross at Calvary and died for my sins, and I am now willing to turn from them.

You said in the Bible that if we confess the Lord Jesus with our mouth and believe in our heart that You raised Him from the dead, we shall be saved.

Right now I confess Jesus as my Lord. With my heart, I believe that God raised Jesus from the dead. This very moment I accept Jesus Christ as my own personal Saviour and according to His Word, right now I am saved.

Amen